Helping Teenagers
Grow Morally

Also by C. Ellis Nelson

How Faith Matures
Where Faith Begins

Edited by C. Ellis Nelson

Congregations: Their Power to Form and Transform

A GUIDE FOR ADULTS

Helping Teenagers Grow Morally

C. ELLIS NELSON

WESTMINSTER/JOHN KNOX PRESS
Louisville, Kentucky

© 1992 C. Ellis Nelson

Scripture quotations are from the New Revised Standard Version of the Bible, copyright © 1989 by the Division of Christian Education of the National Council of the Churches of Christ in the U.S.A., and are used by permission.

Book design by Publishers' WorkGroup

First edition

Published by Westminster/John Knox Press
Louisville, Kentucky

This book is printed on acid-free paper that meets the American National Standards Institute Z39.48 standard. ∞

PRINTED IN THE UNITED STATES OF AMERICA
2 4 6 8 9 7 5 3 1

Library of Congress Cataloging-in-Publication Data

Nelson, Carl Ellis, 1916–
  Helping teenagers grow morally : a guide for adults / C. Ellis Nelson. — 1st ed.
      p.   cm.
  Includes bibliographical references.
  ISBN 0-664-25305-9
  1. Christian education of teenagers.   2. Moral education.
I. Title.
BV1485.N45   1992
241'.0835—dc20   91-45297

Contents

Preface

If you're looking for a book that tells teenagers how to behave, provides solutions to moral problems, or assumes that morals change when individuals think about what they ought to do, you should look elsewhere.

This book is based on the biblical and classical Greek idea that morals are an outgrowth of the kind of society we want, that they are related to beliefs about the meaning of life, which are formed in and sustained by groups of people. Therefore, we must think about how we want to live together in order to make good moral decisions. This view does not reduce individual responsibility in making such decisions, but it does require that we consider the role of society in moral matters.

The social nature of morals creates our major problem in moral education. Morals are formed in us in early childhood by parents and care-giving adults. These adults transmit to small children what they consider right or wrong, good or bad, according to the social group to which they belong. Children rapidly absorb what is said and the moral standards that are modeled in the home, neighborhood, and school. By the age of ten, children have a "moral compass" by which they make decisions. This childhood phase of moral development is extremely important, but I describe these years only as a preparation for understanding adolescents.

The great spurt of physical growth from about eleven or twelve years of age to about sixteen is also a time when individuals develop the ability to reason abstractly. As they move through the teen years, they are increasingly held accountable for their decisions, are expected to prepare for a vocation, and are becoming more self-sufficient. These teen years are of critical importance for moral development; this is the time when the morals acquired in childhood are tested. Peers often propose behavior that is new or has been forbidden. Free to roam beyond family and neighborhood, teenagers see life-styles different from their own. Using their rapidly developing ability to reason and their increased confidence in their own judgment, they often challenge conventional moral standards. This testing in terms of arguing or acting out one's impulses is necessary in order for young people to develop the self they want to be.

Most teenagers are so involved in themselves that we think their moral development is something they do by themselves. Actually, the reverse is true; during the teen years, when young people are testing their beliefs and morals, they are obviously dependent on the groups to which they belong. At no other stage of life do we see such power of peer groups or gangs as during adolescence, when individuals are struggling to free themselves somewhat from their family and move toward the adult groups with which they identify their well-being. This is an anxious period, and teenagers find support and guidance in groups. In these groups they will refine or revise the moral compass they have brought with them from childhood.

According to several recent national polls, a very high percentage of teenagers believe in God and attend church fairly regularly. So congregations have a unique opportunity to be a stabilizing influence and to help teenagers grow morally during their period of transition from the dependence of childhood to the relative independence of adulthood. The question is: How? The answer proposed in this book is: Through teenagers' participation in a congregation as a community concerned about the practice of morals.

This book was written to help adults with this important task. It is intended to be a study book for a *group* of adults, because adults are in charge of congregations and they create the ethos by which it lives. If a group of adults will study this congregational approach to Christian morals and work with their teenagers on common issues, the next generation of church members will be greatly strengthened in faith and morals.

Robert W. Lynn encouraged me to undertake this project and processed a grant through the Lilly Endowment for its development. Craig Dykstra, Daniel Aleshire, and Michael Warren served as advisers. They helped plan the project and criticized the first draft. Ismael Garcia and Prescott Williams, professors at Austin Presbyterian Seminary, and Judy Fletcher, co-pastor of Westminster Presbyterian Church, Houston, Texas, read and critiqued the manuscript. Robert H. Leslie, Jr., senior pastor, and Pamela P. Engler, director of education, at First Presbyterian Church, Bryan, Texas, invited Ray Hinnant, Sherry Hinnant, Norma Funkhouser, Jo Johnston, Ron Cockroft, Jeannette Cockroft, and Vicki Gergeni to use the first draft of this book in a weekly study session. Tape recordings of their comments were invaluable in making revisions. The entire manuscript was read and greatly improved by the careful editorial work of my wife, Nancy. Austin Presbyterian Seminary is a congenial place with excellent resources for research and writing. The seminary also supported the project by providing Dorothy Andrews to type the manuscript and Melba Robbins, a student assistant, to check the references and read the text for errors. My thanks to all these people and to Jack Stotts, president of Austin Presbyterian Seminary, for their encouragement and help.

C. E. N.

May 1991

Helping Teenagers
Grow Morally

CHAPTER 1

Our Moral Nature

This book is for *adults* who are concerned about morals and want to know what they can do as *members of a congregation* to help teenagers acquire moral standards from a Christian perspective.

Two Meanings of "Moral"

The first meaning of the word "moral" is the kind of behavior expected of everyone in a society. This meaning comes from the Latin word *mores*, which means the customs by which people live. Strictly speaking, the word "moral" suggests no particular standard; it simply means that what people in a society believe and practice as correct conduct is right in their view. Thus cannibalism is customary or "right" in tribes that practice it. And in Old Testament times it was "wrong" to accept interest on money a Hebrew lent to a Hebrew (Deut. 23:19–20).

The second meaning of the word "moral" is the kind of behavior a person or group has thought about and considers right, based on some principle or belief that is often different from what society in general expects. This meaning, usually referred to as "ethics," comes from a Greek word and means a critical appraisal of the way people live and the reasons they offer for their behavior. Thus medical doctors or a group of other professional people work out a "code of ethics." Or other groups of people— after careful consideration of the meaning of life—believe they should not kill other human beings and refuse to serve in the Armed Forces.

Unfortunately, the two meanings of the word "moral" are often used interchangeably. This causes considerable confusion. The distinction between the two meanings is of critical importance. A great deal of what we call moral is actually generated by our society and may or may not be in harmony with our Christian faith. Therefore, we must be careful to identify the kind of morals we are discussing in order to maintain the distinctiveness of morals from a Christian perspective.

In order to distinguish the two meanings of the word, I will use terms such as "conventional" or "social" morals to mean the customs by which we live (mores). I will use the word "moral" as we do in ordinary conversation to mean behavior based on principles or beliefs (ethics). People can be moral in this second meaning without being Christian, so it may be necessary at times to use the phrase "Christian morals."

Conventional Morals

Let's start with conventional morals, because they are the pattern of behavior or actions with which almost everyone in a society agrees. Out of its beliefs about life, death, and nature, a society will develop a code of behavior defining what it considers right or wrong. The Inca Indians in South America believed that human sacrifice was necessary for good crops. This belief made such a sacrifice right. We do not hold such a belief and therefore consider human sacrifice wrong. Polygamy is normal and therefore proper in some societies; monogamy, in other societies. A religious society also generates conventional morals based on its beliefs. The Religious Society of Friends (Quakers) believes that the deliberate taking of human life is wrong even in war. Quakers, therefore, will go to jail or perform alternative service rather than be a combatant in military service.

Does this mean that morals are always linked to a society and are true only if a society endorses them? Are there no moral standards for humankind beyond the conventional standards of a particular society? The answer is that some moral standards have emerged in all societies because a society must have order if people are to live in peace and dignity. Certain moral standards such as prohibitions against murder, stealing, lying, and incest are universal.

However, beyond the matter of establishing and maintaining order, a society has beliefs which are expressed in law and custom. Some principles or basic assumptions about human life are universally shared, but the beliefs about how to act on those principles differ from one society to another. The Incas practiced human sacrifice because they believed the sacrifice would bring a good harvest. The underlying moral principle or basic assumption was that all people should have food. Polygamy was the practice in Old Testament times and is still in practice in some societies today. That practice emerges from societies where it is believed that a woman has no place or status apart from a family headed by a man. The underlying moral principle is that women, and by inference children, must be provided for. Likewise, underneath the Quakers' belief in pacifism is the basic assumption that human life is precious and should be protected. Other Christians share that basic assumption but believe there are some circumstances, even certain wars, where taking human life is necessary in order to prevent a worse social condition.

There are, therefore, moral principles, common concerns, or basic assumptions about life that are endorsed by people throughout the world. It is the beliefs about how these basic assumptions can be realized that produce different codes of what is right and wrong. This means our discussion should center on beliefs; for if beliefs change, moral behavior will change. For example, when the Incas understood there was no connection between good crops and human sacrifice, that practice changed.

Morals

The second meaning of moral is behavior based on well-thought-out principles. Such principles range from those endorsed by communist societies to those held by secular groups dedicated to preserving the environment.

This book will use the word "moral" to mean behavior based on well-thought-out principles of the Christian faith. Although this focuses our discussion, it does not provide us with a ready-made answer to moral problems. There are several interpretations of Christian beliefs, and each results in somewhat different ideas about how one should live. In fact, almost every congregation will have within it groups of people who disagree on such moral issues as war, abortion, distribution of wealth, use of drugs and alcohol, civil disobedience, and premarital sexual experience. This book, therefore, does not deal directly with moral issues, because the more fundamental matter is one's beliefs and how those beliefs are translated into behavior. The question is this: How can members of a congregation work through their beliefs and arrive at an agreement about their moral standards?

The answer to that question is itself based on a belief: the belief that, if congregations will work to become a *community of believers*, they will move toward some unity of belief and patterns of behavior or style of life that deal with contemporary moral issues. If such agreement is not possible concerning a particular moral issue, the congregation still remains a place where members can maintain an openness to the leading of God's Spirit about the moral issues on which they disagree.

This thesis—that the congregation is the place where the Christian position is worked out concerning a moral issue—is discussed in the next two chapters.

What About Virtues?

Both meanings of the word "moral" start with a society or a group of people. Are morals not personal? Do they not show up in what we call virtues—that is, individual characteristics such as honesty? Yes, virtues are located in persons.

Virtues are the traits people believe are desirable in order for their society to be what they want it to be. Virtues are values, patterns of behavior, or characteristics the exercise of which causes people to feel good about themselves because they are supporting the beliefs of their society or other social groups to which they give their allegiance. The opposites of virtues are vices—those things that corrupt a society. These cause people to become fearful or uncertain about their future.

Living by a set of virtues may define a "good" person within a society but not necessarily a moral person. The virtues in middle-class American society are well summarized in the Boy Scout Laws: Be trustworthy, loyal, helpful, friendly, courteous, kind, obedient, cheerful, thrifty, brave, clean, and reverent. These virtues come from a stable democratic society based on the Jewish and Christian religions. But many of these virtues also characterize criminal society; the Mafia expects *its* members to be trustworthy as they go about their business of extortion, racketeering, and loan-sharking.

The Mafia also considers loyalty, helpfulness, obedience, and bravery to be absolutely necessary *among its members.* It probably encourages members to be friendly, courteous, kind, and cheerful *to one another* and to develop personal habits of cleanliness. The virtues of a society do not give us a true picture of the morals of a group; we must also identify the *purpose* of the society and the *beliefs* it lives by.

Moral people live by virtues, but they are concerned also about the whole society in which they live. This concern is expressed in a critical analysis of the purpose and characteristics of their society based on their moral principles. Their moral principles combine a vision of how life ought to be lived and a strong desire to create that style of life. In chapter 7 we will discuss five moral principles based on the Christian faith and will identify some specific ethical issues in which a congregation may be involved.

Communities Within a Society

Conventional morals within the United States and Western democratic societies are expressed in laws and customs. Except for criminal organizations such as the Mafia, almost everyone in the nation agrees that conventional morals constitute the way people should behave in order to have the kind of society they want.

Within the nation are many organizations or communities with special beliefs and morals they want to promote. Some of these groups are political parties that want to change some laws and customs. Organizations such as Greenpeace believe wildlife should be protected, so they work to change laws and customs that endanger animals. The National Rifle Association believes everyone has the right to own a gun and lobbies legislatures and Congress to protect that right. Denominations also have special interests and often try to influence Congress or the President by issuing pronouncements about issues they believe to be of moral significance.

The Church Can Influence Society

This situation of communities with their special beliefs and morals working within a society to change that society's conventional morals creates a dynamic situation. The church has an opportunity to shape the beliefs of its members and, through its members, to influence conventional moral standards. An illustration of how this happens is the change in moral standards regarding money-lending.

The Old Testament prohibited the Hebrews from charging interest on money lent to other Hebrews but allowed interest on money lent to others. Christians continued that belief and practice through the first fifteen hundred years of the church. Jews, being able to accept interest on money lent to Christians, became the bankers in the Middle Ages. In reforming beliefs about God and society, John Calvin turned his back on the Old Testament passages forbidding interest on money-lending and on the theologians of the medieval centuries who supported that view. Calvin said—in effect—that the social conditions of the simple agrarian society of the Old Testament and the feudalism of the medieval period were changing. A changed society needed a different morality about interest. He and the Protestant churches he influenced affirmed that accepting interest on borrowed money was morally acceptable and lawful. Calvin, knowing the sinfulness of humankind, put certain conditions on money-lending, such as a limit on the amount of interest, an obligation to lend to the poor at no interest, and a restriction on the security of the loan to the value of the loan. His beliefs became widely accepted in Geneva, Antwerp, London, Amsterdam, and other industrial centers, changing the morals of money-lending and opening the way for the capitalist economic system.[1]

Society Can Influence the Church

Members of churches are also participants in all aspects of our society. As a result, what happens in public life can often influence church members and church beliefs.

For example, developments in science, especially medical science, have influenced the church to reconsider its beliefs about death. Until recent years we believed a person was dead when the heart stopped beating. Now medical science can keep a person nourished and breathing and the heart beating for a long time after the person has lost consciousness. This development in medical science has raised anew the question, "When is a person dead?" The new idea that the person is dead when the brain no longer functions for a specified period of time has gained wide approval. With this definition doctors may stop artificial means of life support and remove organs for transplanting to other people, even though the person is not dead by the older definition.

Here is a second example. Until the middle of this century there was little public discussion of waste disposal. Manufacturing companies disposed of their waste in whatever way was convenient and economical. This was conventional morals; it was the commonly accepted manner of dealing with industrial trash. With the publication of Rachel L. Carson's *Silent Spring* in 1962, the public became aware of how toxic chemicals dumped in the ground or in rivers were appearing in the food we eat. We also learned that toxic fumes from smokestacks entered the air we breathed and united with moisture in the air and rained acid on our forests and food. Radioactive waste material from our atomic plants also became a problem. Everyone feared that, wherever it was placed, it would leak into our water supply. This new view of toxic waste has changed the morality of its disposal. It is no longer "moral" for a company to get rid of toxic waste by any convenient and economical means. We now require that such waste be disposed of or treated in a way that does not harm the environment.

Historical events can also change beliefs of the church, which in turn cause it to change its customs. One of the most significant movements in recent years is the feminist or women's liberation movement. The history of this movement goes back into the nineteenth century, but the two World Wars in the twentieth century and the civil rights movement of the 1960s were the historical events that changed our society's beliefs about the role of women and resulted in a new awareness of their rights. During the later part of the nineteenth century the pressure from women was for greater educational opportunities (many colleges would not admit women), for laws ensuring women's control over their earnings and property, and for their right to vote. A constitutional amendment giving women the vote in national elections was first proposed in 1878. It was proposed every year through 1914 and was defeated every time. But during World War I women served in so many roles and with such valor that public opinion about their rights changed, and the Nineteenth Amendment granting women the right to vote passed in 1920.

World War II provided women opportunities to serve in the branches of the armed services in almost every capacity except actual combat. In civilian life they moved into shipbuilding and many other "masculine" occupations. As a result a whole generation of women became aware of their worth and grew impatient with rules, regulations, and customs that prevented them from the kind of employment they desired, once the war was over.

The women's liberation movement gained strength and broadened its support during the civil rights and anti-Vietnam War protests of the 1960s. Women who participated in those movements learned how to focus public attention on their grievances. The National Organization for Women (NOW), formed in 1966, is one of several organizations established to gain equal rights for women. These organizations raised public consciousness about the second-class status of women in our society. As people came to believe women deserved rights equal to those of men, the rules, regulations, and customs regarding women as candidates for public office, for vacancies on the Supreme Court, and for executives of corporations changed. As the beliefs about the rights of women were being recognized in society, the church also reviewed its treatment of women. Many denominations that previously had not ordained women voted to do so.

The Problem

The situation may be summarized as follows. Morals are the practical expression of what people believe. However, we have two major sets of morals. One set—conventional morals—is based on beliefs we share with everyone in order to have a stable society. The other set—Christian morals—is based on our religious beliefs and is shared within a church. Although the two sets overlap considerably, there is tension between the two because the underlying beliefs are different.

The problem is: To which set of beliefs will we give first allegiance? The way we solve this problem will have a direct bearing on the way we communicate moral standards to our youth. If our first allegiance is to the beliefs and morals of our society, we will let our teenagers absorb the prevailing morals from school, mass media, friends, and community organizations.

This book assumes that our first allegiance is to Christian beliefs. Such an assumption commits us to a biblical strategy first proposed in the Old Testament covenant on Mount Sinai just before the giving of the Ten Commandments. The people of Israel were told that if they would obey God, they would be a holy nation and through them the world would be blessed (Ex. 19:5–6). That is, God's people are to be formed as a community that worships God and seeks to do God's will. The community seeking God's will is apart from, yet concerned about, the larger society. Jesus used the same strategy in selecting and training a small group of followers. The disciples were charged to change the society in which they lived (Matt. 9:35–11:1). Peter used the same strategy when he founded the first Christian congregations (Acts 2:37–47).

Our Solution

If our first allegiance is to Christian beliefs, then our strategy is to develop the congregation into a community where morals are the practical expressions of Christian beliefs. Most of the worship of a congregation—including the sermon, the educational program, and the informal conversations of members—is about practical problems of living; it is therefore about morals.

Every congregation by its very nature fosters a certain moral life-style. The life-style is presented in the lives of saints, in stories, and in songs. One of the most powerful forms of modeling the congregation's image of how a person should live occurs when the congregation—in a worship service or church night supper— recognizes and celebrates a member because that person has done something to demonstrate what the congregation stands for.

This congregational form of setting forth a life-style and supporting it through a variety of means is the best strategy for moral education, especially for teenagers. The congregational model contains the usual "don'ts," such as don't lie, cheat, use drugs, or use violence or force to get what you want. It also promotes love and care for one another as the major Christian virtue. (We'll discuss the full range of virtues and vices in the last chapter.) In addition, the congregation supports a positive program of concern for the community and the world. This aggressive "goodness" is expressed in practical help for the hungry and homeless in the community and in sending missionaries to other places to help with education, agriculture, and health care. Out of all this, many members of a congregation develop what might be called moral wisdom—an ability to discern quickly what is right or wrong in a life situation. These people become known in the congregation, and members often go to them quietly for advice about moral decisions they must make.

Let's look at the civil rights movement and the Mormon Church as illustrations of how powerfully congregations can communicate morals when they act on their beliefs.

Civil Rights

Probably the most fundamental change in American society in the twentieth century has come about through the civil rights movement. Although African Americans were in theory as free as white citizens, at the beginning of this century they were educated in separate schools, lived in segregated neighborhoods, and were prevented from entering most professions. Several organizations were founded in the early part of this century to advance the status of black people, and in 1954 the Supreme Court ruled that public

schools must be desegregated. Many southern states, however, refused to obey the Supreme Court ruling. As a result, a strong civil
rights movement developed to desegregate the schools, secure universal voting rights, and eliminate racial discrimination. Now, toward the end of the twentieth century, African Americans, although
still the object of discrimination, are found in all our schools, are free
to participate in professional sports, are leaders in the Armed Services, work in all professions, serve on the Supreme Court, and
have been elected governors of southern states and mayors of our
largest cities.

The role of Christian churches, especially African American congregations, in the struggle for civil rights during the 1950s and 1960s
is often forgotten. For example, on February 1, 1960, four black teenagers went to Woolworth's lunch counter in Greensboro, North
Carolina; they sat down and ordered food. They were refused service, so they "sat in." After an hour the food counter was closed for
the day.

The idea of a nonviolent request for basic rights spread within
two weeks to fifteen cities in five southern states. Within a year over
fifty thousand students, mostly black, had participated in some kind
of nonviolent demonstrations, and some thirty-six hundred had
spent time in jail. Within a year hundreds of lunch counters were
desegregated in the states bordering the Old South.[2] Historians of
the civil rights movement now judge that this sit-in, which led to the
formation of the Student Nonviolent Coordinating Committee
(SNCC), "injected a more zealous tone" into the civil rights movement when it appeared to be floundering.[3]

This enormous burst of moral activity by teenagers and college
students was a product of black congregations. Students were nourished on Christian beliefs. For example, John Lewis, who was from a
small town in Alabama, happened to be in Nashville as a student
when the sit-ins began. He became involved in this form of nonviolent protest and was jailed on several occasions. His mother wrote
him a letter in which she told him to get out of the movement. In his
reply to her he said, "I have acted according to my convictions and
according to my Christian conscience. . . . My soul will not be satis-
fied until freedom, justice, and fair play become a reality for all people."[4] The adult leaders were all ministers. The congregations were
the places where the students went for support, both spiritual and
physical. Since SNCC students had only $10 a week for living ex-

penses, members of congregations often provided housing and food. During worship the whole congregation shared the suffering and success of the students while they prayed for those who were beaten or jailed for civil disobedience.

Mormons

The civil rights struggle shows the enormous potential of congregations for initiating and sustaining moral activity. But some readers might say this was a onetime thing, a social movement whose time had come, and that congregations are not able to influence teenagers on a regular basis.

The Mormons may be a good illustration of a church with distinctive beliefs and well-defined moral standards. In our day when many teenagers indulge all their appetites, Mormons are able to raise teenagers who abstain from alcohol, tobacco, and coffee. While teenagers in most mainline Protestant denominations drop out of church when they finish high school, Mormon youth spend two years in voluntary missionary work throughout the world at their own expense. When many people look to the government to supply food, rent money, and medical care, Mormons resist government aid. They ask each family to maintain a year's supply of food and clothing for emergencies. Moreover, they support a variety of enterprises and organizations to take care of their members so that Mormons in need are not dependent on government welfare.

The purpose of these comments about the Mormon life-style is not to promote their beliefs but to illustrate the potential of congregational life as a strategy for the moral education of teenagers.

Ordinary Congregations

Can congregations in mainstream denominations resist secular society as African American congregations did in the civil rights movement and as Mormon churches still do? Yes, but the question is: How far can they go? To some extent all congregations go counter to the conventional morals of American society, or they would not be recognized as churches. The issue is: How deliberately does a congregation try to translate its beliefs into moral practices? We will deal with that question in the next chapter.

CHAPTER 2

A Moral Community

The congregation, as the local church in which members participate in face-to-face relationships, has always had a dual citizenship. Its first loyalty is to what Jesus referred to as the kingdom of God; yet the congregation is always influenced by and related to the society in which it is located. The two relationships are difficult to separate, for each influences the other. However, for study purposes, this chapter will look at morals from the standpoint of the congregation's faith in God. The next chapter will examine how the congregation can foster moral decision-making even though its members often disagree about the issues they are considering.

Congregational Responsibility

A congregation is a moral community. This is so because when people meet together and share their experiences over a long period of time, they identify behavior they consider right or wrong. Each congregation will develop characteristics of its own as members talk to one another and as the officers make decisions for its work. The issue, therefore, is what set of beliefs members of a congregation use as they enact their ideas of what is good or bad.

Adults come to congregational life out of a secular world that has its own set of beliefs and moral standards. This secular mentality contains a mixture of many standards and beliefs, some of considerable value for congregations. For example, accountability and efficiency in the handling of money or in the management of property are desirable. Also, some businesses and secular organizations have strict rules for the employment of people regardless of race, gender, age, or physical handicap. But some of the beliefs and morals that adults bring with them need to be challenged from a Christian standpoint. For example, secular society—as displayed in many TV programs, magazine stories of popular singers, and newspaper accounts of many leaders in business and finance—promotes individual achievement as the goal of life. This bottom-line mentality tends to define right and wrong on the basis of success in secular terms. Also, church members, especially teenagers, are well acquainted with the popular belief that one may indulge one's appetite for food, drink, drugs, or sex as long as one "does not hurt someone else."

Given the beliefs and morals adults and teenagers bring with them to congregational worship and work, the congregation must be a place where these beliefs and conventional morals are sorted out. To do so, congregations need to develop and constantly enhance three qualities or characteristics of their life in order to be a moral community based on Christian beliefs: They need to be a true Christian community, to have a concern for moral decision-making, and to provide a place and a time for moral deliberations.

A Christian Community

To be a Christian community means that individuals relate in a special way: Members try to make love of God and care for one another the aim of their association. They want to practice Christian virtues because such virtues strengthen their community. They try to avoid vices that weaken or destroy the fellowship. Members work to accept one another even with all the human weaknesses each person has; at the same time they encourage one another to live more in accord with their beliefs about God.

Because of their religious beliefs, people gather in congregations in order to worship, to have educational programs, to discover service opportunities, and to have fellowship with other Christians. But engaging in these purposes and programs creates conflict. There are always differences of opinion about how to worship and what programs are suitable. There is a struggle to be *in* but not *of* the world. Some members will object to almost any proposal that would change the current work and worship of the congregation.

Given these conditions, what can be done? Often little can be done immediately to ease conflicts, but much can be done about the relationships among people who have differences of opinion. Members of a congregation have as their first responsibility the maintenance of the kind of face-to-face relationship in which members can "speak the truth [as they understand it] in love" in order that all members may become more mature in their understanding of Christ who is the head of the congregation (Eph. 4:15). Thus, the communal characteristics of a congregation make it unique compared to all other human associations and societies. For moral decision-making, the *quality* of the congregation as a Christian community is as important as the issue under discussion (1 Corinthians 14).

Because the congregation is a community, it is different from a denominational decision-making body. Denominations in their regional or national forms are not communities but legislatures. Denominational decision-making practices are designed for administrative matters, such as setting goals, composing official theological statements, and planning national programs. When a denomination deals with moral issues, it often first appoints a committee to study the issue. After a certain amount of discussion, some elected legislative body votes on the study committee's recommendations. Such legislative bodies are in session for a week or so, and most representatives see one another only during that brief period of time. The next meeting of the denomination's legislative body will probably have a different set of elected representatives. Such denominational legislatures are necessary in order to achieve some consensus about national affairs, but the people who make the decisions usually do not know one another very well, do not relate to one another in face-to-face relations over a long period of time, and do not have an obligation to maintain themselves as a community.

This description of denominational decision-making does not depreciate that process. There is no other democratic way to arrive at a national consensus about a moral issue. But we should not confuse the denomination's legislative process—where votes are final—with the slow, conversational, hesitant process of a congregation. Since the congregation is a community, it has an obligation to respect the beliefs of each member and to help members live together in harmony in spite of differences in beliefs and morals.

A Concern for Moral Decision-Making

Next in importance to the communal nature of the congregation is the *basis* on which the congregation makes decisions. The criterion for Christian decision-making is the will of God for the issue at hand. The criterion is not the standards of the community, or the application of moral principles, but: What are Christians to do about the matter because of their faith in God?[1]

What is important about this criterion is our mental image of God, for that image dictates what we think God desires. Our image of God from biblical and historical sources indicates that God is always creating the future. Since the future is unknown, we have only our faith to guide us as we struggle to understand what God intends. But our hope about the future is guided by the record we have of God's guidance in the past. This record is primarily the Bible, but history since New Testament times is of considerable help in showing how those early Christians attempted to discern and do God's will for their day. The past, therefore, shapes a mental image of a God who is concerned about the conditions of human life and affirms that God's will can be known to those who seek it.

This means seeking the will of God is a dynamic process in which we must be constantly engaged. Jesus placed this task in the context of prayer. If prayer is the most profound expression of our faith, then, as Jesus instructed us, seeking the will of God is our first request. When asked by the disciples to teach them to pray, Jesus gave them the model prayer we repeat as our basic expression of faith. After the address to God as "Our Father" and an ascription of praise, "hallowed be your name," Jesus said that our first concern should be to ask that God reign over our lives and that God's will be done on earth as it is done in heaven (Matt. 6:9–13; Luke 11:1–4). By placing a concern for doing God's will first in prayer, Jesus affirms that this criterion for decision-making is expected to be used for the practical matters in which we are involved.

It is extremely important to understand that a congregation is to engage in *practicing* moral decision-making on the basis of trying to do the will of God. Decision-making on this basis involves three matters that make it unique.

First, practicing decision-making means that the congregation (or one of its parts, such as the officers, an adult class, or a youth group) is dealing with an issue that will not go away. It is something about which individuals or a group must decide, one way or another. Decision-making about life situations is different from making moral judgments. Moral judgments are made in the mind and result in opinions that may not deal with all the facts and feelings of a real-life situation. Moral decisions are our best efforts to do the right thing under certain conditions. Because a moral decision results in an effort to change the situation, we are deeply concerned with the outcome in order to know whether we judged the conditions properly, how people responded to our actions, and whether the situation is better as a result of our decision. Thus, moral decisions automatically feed back information that may affect future decisions.

Second, decision-making in a Christian community is often tentative. This is so because the people who make up the congregation have different ideas of God's will. Even after careful discussion and persistent prayer, equally qualified and dedicated Christians may disagree about what should be done. Thus a church group may have to make a tentative decision or a decision that will be reviewed and revised later in the light of experience.

The first major conflict in the Christian church ran along these lines. Some Christians in Judea said people could not be saved unless they first obeyed the customs of the Jews. Paul and Barnabas said that one could become a Christian by faith in Christ without following the customs of the Jews. This debate became so serious that representatives of the two points of view went to Jerusalem to have the matter settled by the apostles and elders (Acts 15:1– 21).

Third, decision-making in the community is often a compromise. In the illustration from the book of Acts, the decision was made by the apostles after a thorough discussion of the issue. It was officially a compromise—holding on to a few customs of the Jews but not the major one the Christians from Judea wanted. But the formula, worked out to keep harmony in the church, is not mentioned again, so it seems to have been more of a face-saving arrangement than a compromise. However, it is important to note that the decision-makers went as far as they could to hold the church together as a community and still follow the beliefs of Paul, Peter, and Barnabas —that Gentiles could become Christians without first having to become Jews.

We should also remember that the New Testament church accepted some conditions that were considered wrong. Jesus, for example, is quoted as tolerating divorce even though he judged it wrong (Matt. 5:31–32; 19:8–9).

A Place and a Time for Moral Deliberations

The congregation as a Christian community provides at least three places where moral deliberations can take place.

Deliberation can take place first of all in the worship services and in celebration of the sacraments. These events are not designed to be arenas of moral decision-making, yet they function in that way because they often influence people in the depths of their being to live more in accord with the moral standards of the church and the image they have of Jesus and his teachings. Often people come to worship with an unsolved moral dilemma uppermost in their thoughts. During the service something will click in their minds so that the action they must take becomes clear. This place of decision-making does not mean that worship should be oriented to moral issues; it only means that worship leaders should realize that such a process is going on and provide the proper solemnity and silence for such meditation.

Deliberation should also take place in classes and groups where informal educational processes make it possible to deal with moral issues on a regular basis. Because of the critical role the adults play in the congregation, adult classes need to be deliberate about the selection and discussion of moral issues. They should do so with the understanding that they should share their faith in relation to practical problems, for they are responsible for the quality of the congregation's spiritual life.

The adults of a congregation set the spiritual tone. Their interpretation of the Christian faith results in the mission of that congregation, how much money is contributed and how it is spent, the kind of minister called, what issues will be allowed to come before the congregation, and all other matters that affect the life and work of the congregation. The adults' interpretation of Christianity will be communicated to one another in informal conversations, to their children in their homes, and to their community through their workplaces and other associations.

Finally, deliberation must take place in officers' meetings. The officers of a congregation have a special responsibility for moral decision-making in relation to their particular duties. It may be easier to raise moral issues in officers' meetings than it is in an adult class, because the agenda is made up of matters that need to be decided. In that context, the criterion for decision-making is usually stated by the person who proposes a motion and by those who debate the issue. Issues related to the mission of the congregation, the compensation of staff, the budget, and the use of buildings and equipment will come to the official board for decision.

Too often the board merely decides to do what it did the previous year. Should the official board continue the policies and programs that were approved in the past? Much can be said for the stability of tradition, and past actions should be the starting point for almost all policy discussions. But the reasons for past actions need to be constantly reviewed before decisions are made for the future. For example, salaries of church staff—especially the janitor—are often below comparable salaries in the community. If this is true, why is it so and should it continue to be so? Also, officers often approve a certain curriculum for the church school as they did in the past without a discussion of its present appropriateness for their congregation.

In addition to raising the "why" questions so as to get at the reasons for administrative decisions, official boards need to realize that if they are to take their responsibility for moral leadership seriously, they must devote more time to their work. Too often motions are made and passed about matters that have serious moral implications without taking time for reflection. Time may be the most underused and underappreciated element in decision-making by official boards. A matter of serious moral import should be considered by committees in advance; if there is not a rather large majority in favor of its recommendation, it should be held over to another meeting so everyone will have time to ponder and pray about the proposal.

Individual Responsibility

This chapter began with the observation that adults and teenagers come to the congregation out of a secular world that influences their beliefs and morals. The role of the congregation is to help members identify and evaluate their beliefs in relation to Christian beliefs and morals. This is a slow and difficult process. It was this way in New Testament times also. Peter, who came from a Jewish background, had difficulty sloughing off some of his Jewish moral practices when he became a Christian (Acts 10:28). The apostle Paul had similar problems with some of his converts who came to Christianity from a Greek background (1 Corinthians 8).

This congregational process of helping individuals become more attuned to the will of God than to the ways of the world is essential because Christian faith is personal. The way individuals interpret and live their faith has a direct bearing on the spiritual life of a congregation, on their influence in the workplace, and on their voting for public officials.

The morals of Christian people who are in a community of believers have three characteristics that distinguish them from individuals who make moral decision based on their own interests.

First, the individual is accountable to God. This orientation requires Christians to consider what God's interests are in a moral situation. Thus, the arena for decision-making is not oneself but God's will. Understanding God's will for a specific moral situation is difficult, but to ask what it is and try to answer the question is to bring into the decision-making a power and will outside oneself. One has to consult the Bible and history to find clues to God's interests in the matter at hand. Such consultation provides a perspective beyond the interest of the moment by which to make a decision.

This stance helps individuals transcend the pressure from within to make a self-serving decision, for one is accountable to God and not to one's own interests and wants. This stance also helps one to withstand pressure from people who want to influence the decision for their own interests.

We have many biblical stories of people facing moral decisions who looked to God for guidance and resisted their own self-centered desires or pressures from the outside to conform to what society wanted. Isaiah's invitation to live according to God's ways (55), Amos's indictments against the easy moral practices of Israel (3– 6), or Micah's demands that the people live by their faith (6:1– 8) are but a few examples. Jesus provided us with the finest example when he went to the garden of Gethsemane to pray just before the crucifixion. This was a last review of his options. Jesus prayed, "Father, if you are willing, remove this cup from me; yet, not my will but yours be done" (Luke 22:42).

Second, the individual is responsible for the spiritual quality of the congregation. Christians are accountable to God, but they live in relation to one another in congregations. We have no record in the New Testament of individuals standing alone in their worship or work. All our records are of Christians in congregations. These records attribute to the congregation special spiritual qualities. The congregation is the body of Christ, and Christ, the head, directs the parts (1 Corinthians 12). In Ephesians, Paul repeats this figure of speech (1:23) and also considers the congregation as the temple of God (2:20–22) and the bride of Christ (5:23–32). He understands the church to be the place where the Spirit of Christ functions to "build up" the body of Christ—a community where individual Christians become mature as they practice living by Christian morals (Ephesians 4).

This understanding of the individual Christian's obligation to work and worship within a group of fellow Christians includes moral decision-making. The congregation is an immediate source of help and guidance. There one can share moral problems, test solutions with kindred minds, and receive emotional support while going through the anxiety of decision-making. This does not mean that decisions made in the context of a congregation will always be good or right; this will depend on the congregation and its understanding of itself. However, the possibility of making a good moral decision is greatly enhanced when a Christian discusses the matter with others in the congregation.

Third, the individual is concerned about the relation of moral decisions to the good of society. As noted in chapter 1, the congregational approach to morals commits us to a biblical strategy. Congregations are to be communities formed by beliefs, but they are to be both an example to and active in deciding the character of the larger society.

This means, as pointed out in chapter 1, that Christian virtues are more than personal traits. They are to form a society that stands for certain principles. We will discuss those principles in chapter 7. At this point we note that people who are "good" by *conventional* moral standards do not always form a good society. The race relations situation in the United States was used in chapter 1 to illustrate this point. Before the struggle for civil rights in the 1950s and 1960s, many Christian white people treated blacks justly in personal relations. Yet during that time racial inequality was legal in education and was practiced in employment and in most social relations. It was not until racial equality was applied to society by law that public schools were integrated and employment opportunities were guaranteed regardless of race. The same can be said of recent changes regarding employment of women and older people. It was not until the moral principles of fairness were applied to society and were expressed in laws that people in these groups could have the same employment opportunities as young white males.

This characteristic of Christian persons wanting to help form the policies of the larger society creates serious problems for a congregation. Members will have deep differences of opinion about public policy issues. Do owners of natural resources have the right to use them as they desire? Who controls such resources as the ocean and the air? On what basis should the government make tax decisions? These and similar questions have thoughtful but different answers. Seldom can the congregation as a whole community come to agreement about such matters. There is, however, a way for Christians to deal with these matters by considering morals to be a "practice." We will explore this idea in the next chapter.

CHAPTER 3

A Practice
of Moral Living

The faith of the church, as indicated in chapter 2, orients people to God. The more a congregation attends to its citizenship in the kingdom of God, the more it becomes a unique community, different from the surrounding society. However, the congregation is also a social institution deeply influenced by the society of which it is a part. This institutional aspect of the congregation creates serious ethical problems.

Institutional Religion

If religion is to endure from one generation to the next, it must become institutionalized. This means its beliefs will be formalized so they can be taught and explained, a distinct form of worship will emerge, membership requirements will be established, and a plan for the selection of leaders will be recognized. Some Christian groups, such as the Quakers, have an informal institutional structure. Others, such as the Roman Catholic and Eastern Orthodox churches, have developed an elaborate structure. From the beginning the Christian church had an organization with procedures for the selection of officers. Before the close of the New Testament era, Christianity had an institutional form including ordination of ministers, style of worship, sacraments, requirements for membership, and some coordination of work and sharing of money among congregations.

The institutional form of Christianity is the carrier of faith, but it is not the same as faith in God. Faith in God is based on an experience with Jesus Christ. This experience leads one to congregate with others who have had a similar experience in order to understand the experience, to worship God, and to work for God's concerns in the world. The congregation is therefore a means to an end, not an end in itself. This subordination of the institutional church to its mission is easy to discuss but difficult to achieve. We know faith needs an institutional form to endure, so the temptation is to pay attention to the institution rather than to the faith it represents.

This tension between faith in God and the institution that is to preserve, interpret, and promote the faith runs all through the Bible. Probably the most brilliant Old Testament expression of this issue is found in the prophets, especially Amos, who quotes the Lord as saying, "I hate, I despise your festivals, and I take no delight in your solemn assemblies" (Amos 5:21). Why? Because Israel has forgotten that the purpose of festivals and assemblies is the establishment of justice and a concern to be right with God (Amos 5:21–24; see also Micah 6:6–8). According to Matthew's gospel, Jesus blasted the scribes and pharisees (who were among the Jewish religious leaders of his time) because they did not practice what they preached. These leaders were more concerned with the institution of religion—rules of conduct, proper garments, special privileges and recognition for leaders, proper procedures in worship, and glorification of past prophets—than they were about their relation to God (Matthew 23). The books of the New Testament written at the end of that era show an institutional church struggling with this same problem. For example, James writes that church ushers must not pay more attention to the seating of wealthy men than to a poor man in shabby clothing (Jas. 2:1–7).

The tension between faith in God and concern for the church as an institution continues. Because there are serious ethical problems related to this tension, we need to examine it in more detail. The reasons for the tension fall generally into four categories.

First, the congregation is a social institution. It is designed to continue to exist beyond the life or influence of any one person or any small group of people. In order to function as an institution, it has a purpose and a program, rules for people joining or leaving, a governance for leadership selection and decision-making, a standard of behavior for members, and means of legal approval and responsibility for owning property. As a social institution, it has a strong desire to maintain itself and to enhance its reputation in the community. Thus, every one of the characteristics of the congregation as an institution may stand in tension with the Christian faith. For example, its purpose and program may cater to the wishes of the members as a social club does: Its rules for entrance into membership may exclude or discourage the poor or people of other races, its governance may be intolerant of diverse opinion, its standards of behavior my be too rigid or too lax, and it may prevent worthwhile community organizations from using its property.[1]

Second, the purpose of the congregation is not commonly agreed upon. Although members of a congregation have enough in common to worship and work together, almost all congregations will have members who disagree about its purpose. Some think of the church as primarily an enlarged family where their values are celebrated and taught. Others will have a mental image of the congregation as a local unit of a great historical tradition, such as Lutheran, Presbyterian, or Roman Catholic. Other members will consider the church to be a religious organization dedicated to serving or challenging the practices of the community in which they live. Still others will think of the church primarily in evangelistic terms and will want to focus attention on those who have not made a confession of faith.[2] Because members have different understandings of the purpose of the congregation, they will disagree when issues arise about how to spend the available money, what kind of buildings are needed, or what should be the qualifications of the employed staff.

Third, the program and pronouncements may not suit all members. Differences of opinion about the purpose of the church just mentioned also produce tension about the work of the congregation. Most church members tolerate disagreements about the activities of the congregation by not cooperating or by refusing to fund what they do not like. This produces the ethical/theological problem of loyalty. If people are loyal to Christ as head of the church, they will discuss their differences and attempt to play down their own interests in order to find the "mind" of Christ for the whole congregation (Phil. 2:1–18). But church members live in the secular world, and they often use its secular standards of judgment for the work of the congregation. Some church members have accepted uncritically the "success" standard, and they judge to be "right" whatever increases membership or improves the financial strength of the congregation. Others may have become enamored of psychological health and feel that whatever the congregation does to help people "feel good" about themselves must be promoted.

Fourth, the people may not live up to the moral standards they profess. This condition was stated in an unforgettable way by Paul: "So I find it to be a law that when I want to do what is good, evil lies close at hand" (Rom. 7:21). The tension between what we know we should do and what we actually do because of selfish desires, impulses to satisfy our bodily needs, lack of concern for other people, impatience, love of money, lure of prestige, and similar motives is with us constantly. Everyone—inside and outside the church—understands this tension. If Christians admit the tension between their moral ideals and their actual practices and show a sincere effort to live by their ideals, there is little to criticize. However, if Christians ignore this tension, their moral standards will become laws and goodness will become legalistic. The Sermon on the Mount is Jesus' explanation of the difference between faith in God and a legalistic interpretation of religion (Matthew 5–7).

Practicing Morals

The usual explanation for the tension between what the church actually does in its life and work and the moral standards its professes is that the church is a human institution subject to sin and human mistakes. This is a correct explanation, but it restricts morals to sin and forgiveness. Morals involves thinking about what we ought to say and do in all life situations because we are Christian, and this is a much bigger problem.

Of the four areas of tension just mentioned, only the fourth is directly related to sin. Although sin and human weaknesses are involved in the first three, there are other matters to be considered. For example, all human institutions--including the government, the public schools, and the law courts—fail to live up to their self-selected ideals just as a church fails to do so. The moral issue is how can the church better embody its beliefs? The purpose of the church is a matter on which equally committed Christians can differ; the moral issue is whether the members can maintain their community even if they disagree. The program and pronouncements of the church do not suit every member's needs; the moral issue is whether the members will try to help one another find Christian solutions to their problems.

Alasdair MacIntyre has proposed a way of thinking about our moral life apart from its institutional sponsor. MacIntyre thinks of the moral decision-making of a community as a "practice." A practice is all that goes on in a community of people who have agreed on goals to be reached and what constitutes excellence in trying to reach those goals. The game of football is a practice. There is a community of people who agree on what the game is about and what the rules are, who have a memory of past games, and who understand what makes excellence in football. Throwing a football or making a tackle is a skill, not a practice.

The rewards of playing football can be explained only in terms of playing the game, and they can be recognized and appreciated only by those who are in the community that understands and appreciates the game. Players receive personal satisfaction when they show excellence and help the team compete well or win. Their excellence becomes part of the common lore of the game and is used to instruct and inspire other players. Players get public recognition for excellence, but these rewards and prizes all relate to how well they have played the game.[3]

A practice is related to a group of people and exists before the development of institutions related to the practice. Football was a game played for fun and recreation before it became a professional sport and was then institutionalized in the National Football League. Institutionalized football—either professional or sponsored by colleges—is concerned with maintaining the authority of the institution, standardizing and spreading the influence of the game, regularizing and enforcing rules, and all kinds of administrative matters that enhance the glory of the sport. Football as a game can exist without the National Football League, but the NFL cannot exist without football.[4]

Perhaps medicine is a better illustration, because the term "practice of medicine" is in general use. Medical doctors practice according to knowledge, experience, procedures held in common, and their commitment to beliefs about the value of health. Decisions made in this practice are self-correcting, because the doctors involved are dealing with one another in a community held together by their beliefs. Their experience of working together with common understanding is the authority for their practice.

The institutions related to the practice of medicine are hospitals and state and national medical associations. The practice of medicine and the hospitals are designed to support each other; yet the two are different. This distinction between a practice and the institutions related to a practice is an important one for Christians making moral judgments. The religious "practice" is a community of Christians who are concerned to make decisions for current life situations in a faithful manner. The church is the institution. It is wonderful when the church and Christian practice are identical. But the church often acts as an institution by making decisions to protect itself or to advance its prestige in society rather than according to its beliefs.[5]

We have sometimes seen tension because a group in a congregation disagrees with the official position of the congregation. An adult class might, on the basis of its practice of faith, want to adopt a refugee family from a foreign country, even though the congregation as a whole disapproves of this project. The adult class could accomplish its goal by simply making all the necessary arrangements on an informal basis without involving the congregation in an official way.

The idea of Christian practice as distinct from the institutionalized church is important for two reasons. First, it demonstrates the power and priority of the beliefs of the community over its institutional forms. This means that a Christian community—be it a whole congregation or a part, such as a youth group or an adult class— must ask and discuss the critical question: What are we Christians to do about the matter at hand because of our faith in God? This criterion for making moral decisions requires individuals in a community to express what they actually believe, to have those beliefs supported, challenged, or modified by equally sincere fellow Christians, and to be prepared to carry out what they say is morally right. Moral decision-making under these conditions is more like the decisions we make in a family than like decisions made in an institution. Such decisions come from the whole person, not just from the mind. Since they involve a person in ongoing human relationships, the decisions become a part of the person making the decisions and therefore help that person grow spiritually.

Second, this idea of Christian practice also provides a community of understanding and an expectation of what is good and what is right behavior in various circumstances. We have said that morals are the understandings a group of people have about the way they should relate to one another. Different human groupings—such as a work group, school association, social club, or church—hammer out standards of behavior acceptable to their particular group.

What is important about this natural human way to create codes specifying what is right or wrong is the affiliation a person has with the group that creates and maintains the code. If people have a strong positive affiliation with the group where they discuss what is right and wrong behavior in many kinds of life situations, those people develop a mental image of what that group would approve or disapprove. This mental image goes away with them and becomes the reference for all decisions. If the group was meaningful, a person may use the mental image of what the group would approve or disapprove as a standard long after being separated from the group.[6]

The psychology of reference groups applies with special force to church groups. This is so because church groups are naturally communal. People share life experiences, and they work together in various enterprises with noble purposes. Moreover, in small groups or in formal worship services people turn their attention to God through prayer, song, litany, scripture, and sermon. Out of all this comes an image of what Christian groups would approve or disapprove. If a person has a strong positive relationship with a Christian group, the image of what that group considers right and wrong behavior will be that person's guide when away from the group.

Learning by Involvement

If a congregation is consciously trying to be a community of believers who constantly raise questions as to what should be said or done because they are Christian, it is an extremely important place for teenagers to be. This is so because teenagers (1) are beginning to use reason about their religion and (2) need a social environment where they can observe adults struggling with significant moral issues.

Development of Reasoning Abilities

Teenagers as described in the next two chapters come of age under the influence of the moral standards of the community in which they grow up. Even if the standards are those of an excellent Christian community, they were absorbed without critical analysis because children are not capable of such thinking. This does not mean children cannot be kind and generous; it only means they have not developed mentally to the place where they can evaluate what they are doing. In fact, some of the most essential elements of religious morality are established in childhood. A person's reverence for God, respect for the rights of others, acceptance by and appreciation by others, and sympathy for the welfare of others are all started, nurtured, and given meaning during childhood.

Children can be religious, but they cannot be theologically Christian. To be theologically a Christian, individuals must be able to reason about their faith. This ability to think in abstract terms and to put human situations in historical perspective develops during the middle adolescent years, roughly equivalent to the four years of high school. Jerome Kagan shows the change from childhood thinking to adult reasoning with the following illustration. If you said to seven-year-old children, "All three-legged snakes are purple; I'm holding a three-legged snake—guess its color," the children would be confused and probably not answer because the idea of a three-legged snake violates their knowledge of snakes. If you said the same thing to young adolescents, they would probably laugh at the odd idea but would answer correctly because they can separate themselves from a problem and deal with it according to the logical rules that apply. Kagan then shows how this new mental ability expands in the early teen years so that individuals are able to classify things even though their characteristics may contradict appearances. A whale, for example, is a mammal because it has a backbone and nurses its babies, even though it lives in the water and looks like a large fish. Teenagers are increasingly able to think about a variety of factors that affect an event and to make judgments about how those variations affect the outcome. A football game, for example, can depend on the weather (temperature, wind, rain), how a team feels about the opposing team, the health of key players, and so forth. Teenagers spend a lot of time using and developing these mental abilities when they discuss sports and social events.

As teenagers' minds become more mature, they consciously apply their expanding mental ability to religion and morals. Kagan reports that, at the sophomore and junior levels of high school, teenagers are troubled when asked to put these three propositions together:

1. God loves human beings.
2. The world contains many unhappy people.
3. If God loved human beings, God would not make so many people unhappy.[7]

This set of propositions is a teenage version of the unsolved problem of the Jewish and Christian religions: If God is good why does God allow bad things to happen to those who are trying to be faithful to God? No resolution of these conflicting statements is completely satisfactory. One can abandon belief in God or live with the contradiction as Job did; or one can make the response of Jesus when he was asked if a man's blindness was linked to sin, either his or his parents'. The blindness was unrelated to sin, Jesus said. Since no rational explanation of the presence of evil was possible, Jesus advised his followers to use such situations to display their faith in God and to minister to the victims of tragic events (John 9:1–12; see also Matt. 5:45 and Luke 13:1–5).

Teenagers have trouble with the problem of evil because for the first time in their lives they can understand the problem and the difficulties with each response. As they use their newly acquired mental ability with other life situations, they begin to question many of the beliefs and moral standards brought from their childhood. Adults should look on this time when teenagers probe the meaning of beliefs and morals as a great opportunity. It is an opportunity for adults to have conversations with teenagers about their faith, to influence the congregation to provide good leaders for youth groups, and to provide opportunity for teenagers to reformulate their beliefs.

Need for a Social Environment

All age groups need the emotional support of a congregation of like-minded people, but teenagers have special needs during this transition to adulthood. These special needs are (1) a community where they are accepted and respected as persons moving into adulthood and (2) a place where they can observe and practice making moral decisions with adults.

The communal aspect of the congregation is of utmost importance to teenagers. They know they are in a state of transition. They have abandoned their childhood and their neighborhood play group. They are now probably attending a large comprehensive high school and selecting their own group of friends. They are becoming more aware of tensions within themselves, related to questions like "Who am I?" and "What kind of work do I want to do?" They are testing their interests in sports, music, school studies, art, and the other interests to which people devote their lives. All these internal, self-generated problems cause a certain amount of anxiety because they do not know the answers to questions they are asking and they realize no one can answer the questions for them. Lacking experience by which to make judgments about themselves, they have to endure uncertainty until they have tested their abilities and interests.

The anxiety that develops from peer pressure is easy to identify but more difficult to handle. Peers, either in large groups at sports or musical events or in small groups of friends, are always testing. They are testing what they see adults do and the boundaries within which they must live. Because teenagers have freedom to be away from home and the community where they are known, they have the opportunity to use drugs and alcohol, experiment with sex, or try shoplifting, among other things.

Teenagers need a community of people who care about them and respond to their questions and on whom they can depend if they get in trouble. Where can teenagers find such a community? Schools and clubs provide stimulation and fellowship, but such organizations are not dedicated to helping individuals fashion a life. A congregation is the most accessible institution in the community dedicated to helping its members achieve a life of integrity and meaning. A congregation should not try to be different because of the needs of teenagers. It should try to fulfill its mission of being a community in which members are concerned about and care for one another. In such a community teenagers will feel accepted and respected while they are sorting out and dealing with the tensions in their lives.

In addition to being a support to people who are going through personal struggles, a congregation is a place where moral decisions are being made. This feature of congregational life is of critical importance for teenagers.

Although teenagers' eyes are on the adult world into which they are moving, their experience is restricted to home, church, community groups, and school. Community groups and youth clubs often provide excellent experiences in music, sports, nature study, and other interests. Participation in these groups may have positive values, such as helping young people learn the discipline needed to complete any worthwhile project, achieving high standards of performance, or testing their interests. Public high schools— with their attendance rules, required courses, secular orientation, large size, and hierarchical control through impersonal administration—are not set up to relate beliefs to life situations. Moreover, the typical high school adds to the fragmentation of experience. School subjects are treated as fields of study just as they are in college. Unless a student has a course in ethics—which is rarely offered—or a literature or social studies teacher who raises questions about how people should act, public schools do not help students make sense out of the experiences they are having or the events taking place around them.

These comments about community groups and public schools do not mean that these institutions are without moral standards or influence; they have both. But their orientation is to the community at large and reflects conventional moral standards. In contrast, a congregation is oriented to God's will and—if taken seriously—often goes counter to prevailing public opinion or to the values of society. The primary concern of community organizations and public schools is general education that helps teenagers develop special interests. In contrast, the congregation is concerned to be a caring community that is constantly trying to relate its beliefs to life situations.

These characteristics of a congregation—a caring community concerned to relate beliefs to life situations—is exactly what teenagers need. They have (or almost have) the mental ability of adults, but they lack experience in making ethical decisions. If they are in a congregation where members care for and about one another, they will have the support they need while they test new ideas, question beliefs formed in childhood, and deal with peer pressures.

The matter of relating beliefs to life situations must be a deliberate concern of the congregation in order to be effective. Young people are alert to what is said from the pulpit, to announcements about interests and projects supported by the officers, and to what leaders and officers say. If what they hear from these sources helps them relate faith to life experiences, they will listen. The congregation can also arrange to include teenagers in various parts of its work where decisions have to be made based on the beliefs of the church. For example, a representative from the youth group could serve as a member of the budget committee. There the teenager could participate in the struggle to serve God's concerns yet understand the financial restrictions the congregation faces. In fact, to have teenagers serving on almost any of the regular committees of the church will put them in contact with adults who are functioning in the zone between what they would like to do and what they are able to do. Through this experience, teenagers will come to understand how ethical decisions are made in the light of the Christian faith.

CHAPTER 4

Coming of Age
—Social Setting

$\mathbf{L}$et's pause for a moment to recall what has been said so far. In chapter 1, Christian morals were distinguished from conventional morals by the beliefs on which they were based. Although the two sets of morals overlap, a congregation that practices the standards it teaches can have tremendous influence on the morals of children and youth.

Chapter 2 discussed the responsibility of a congregation to be self-consciously Christian in its moral decision-making. If this goal is carefully followed, members will develop a Christian form of individual morality.

Chapter 3 addressed the problem of the congregation as a human institution that falls short of the beliefs it professes. By thinking of morals as a "practice," members of a congregation could carry on a lively moral discourse. If teenagers were involved in these discussions because they were becoming adult in their mental abilities, they would acquire first-hand experience in moral decision-making.

We must not assume, however, that participation in congregational life is sufficient for moral growth. Morals during adolescence are very complicated, for they are also related to social conditions and the way individuals become conscious of themselves as they enter adulthood. In this chapter we will explore the way the social setting influences moral development. In the next chapter we will consider the psychology of self-formation.

Society Defines Adolescence

Biological maturity does not take very long. Although there is wide variation—according to climate, race, gender, and health—as to

35

when the spurt in growth takes place, most of the increase in height and weight occurs in about two years and the whole process is accomplished in about four years. For the average girl the process starts somewhere between the ages of nine and ten, and for boys it starts between the ages of eleven and twelve.

Primitive societies recognize the change of status from childhood to adulthood and determine when formal acknowledgment is to take place. Puberty rites vary greatly from tribe to tribe, but the ceremony does not take long, often a matter of weeks. The children know from those who have gone through the ceremony what to expect—a scarring of the skin, the extraction of a tooth, or some other mark to show that one has passed into adult status. During the puberty rites children will learn the secrets of the tribe, but everything else they already know. They know the lore of the tribe, the kinds of work assigned to men and women, what kind of behavior is approved or disapproved, and who has authority to make tribal decisions. Moreover, the skills they need for life—such as the gathering and preparation of food, how to hunt or fish, proper participation in tribal ceremonies—they have practiced all through childhood. Under these conditions, no teen years are needed to get ready for adulthood.

When we move from tribal societies to Third World countries with an economy based on agriculture, we see that the adolescent years are brief also. Societies of this type expect children to enter into adult work around the age of thirteen or fourteen because advanced education is not required and there is not enough wealth to sustain idle teenagers. It is not unusual to see young boys as soldiers in newspaper pictures of Third World nations at war. Young adolescents in these societies are expected to do what adults do, so the boys are recruited for military service.

American Society About 1900

Before the Civil War, American society was similar to Third World countries today. A small class of well-educated people supplied the lawyers, ministers, medical doctors, and civic leaders. The rest of the population was engaged in farming, hunting, fishing, lumbering, and similar work or in small industries related to those occupations. In 1850 only 15 percent of the population lived in urban areas. In that rural society, by the age of fourteen or fifteen people had all the formal education they needed and all the skills required to undertake adult responsibilities.

After the Civil War, America became more industrialized. By 1880 a national railroad network was in place. Many people moved to urban areas, where manufacturing was centered. In just one decade, 1880 to 1890, the number of cities with a population of more than 8,000 doubled.

By 1900 about 40 percent of the population was living in urban areas. The United States was at the beginning of a rapid expansion in the manufacture of automobiles, farm machinery, boats, and steam engines of many kinds and in the construction of roads and bridges, telegraph lines, and everything connected with the generation and use of electricity. By the beginning of World War I the United States was capable of manufacturing all the implements of war, including airplanes. The move to the cities continued. The 1920 census showed that 51 percent of Americans were living in urban centers.

The rapid industrialization of America required a large number of people with education more advanced than was necessary when the nation was primarily agricultural. More education required more time in the teen years for schooling, and industrialization produced enough wealth to support teenagers while they attended school. Thus at the beginning of this century we began to develop what today we call the "teen years" or "youth" as a period of time in which individuals are no longer children but are not yet adults.

The move toward an industrial society changed the way people lived, and this created social conditions that had to be regulated by laws stipulating compulsory education and the age at which people could be employed. These laws defined and called attention to the emerging "youth" stage of life.

Although schools, especially those for children, were always available in America, it was not until the 1830s that states, following the leadership of Massachusetts, began to establish a free public school system. The movement for compulsory education in state schools developed after the Civil War. By 1900, thirty-two states had passed laws requiring attendance at public school between the ages of seven or eight and fourteen. In 1890 there were 4,158 high schools with 297,894 students; in 1930 there were 26,690 high schools with an enrollment of 4,740,580. During this forty-year period the population doubled, but high school enrollment increased sixteen times! By 1930 a high school diploma was not only the expected level of educational attainment for everyone; it was also necessary for most of the jobs in industrial society.

Child labor laws also helped to define the teen years. The labor of children, usually in the ten-to-fifteen-year range, was common all through the 1800s. By 1900 the use of child labor began to decrease, because of the opposition of organized labor and of public school officials and because about half the states had laws restricting child labor. As the nation became more industrialized after 1900, more states passed laws setting the age at which a teenager could be employed. These laws—which were in harmony with the school attendance laws—produced a larger number of well-educated people for a society that had become much more complex. By 1938 a national law, upheld by the Supreme Court, defined the age at which teenagers could work. From the age of fourteen to sixteen they could be employed after school, at sixteen they could work full time, but they had to be eighteen for certain hazardous occupations.

These brief comments about the way a period of time in the life cycle was lengthened and labeled "adolescence" or "youth" as a result of the industrialization of the United States should be supplemented with a few observations about the way churches and Christian leaders responded to this emerging new stage of life. Francis Clark, a minister in Boston, saw a growing number of young people congregating in the city, so he formed Christian Endeavor in 1881 for their special interest. This organization grew rapidly because "youth" as an extended period of time was developing throughout the Northeast, and the traditional Sunday school class was not adequate for young people's spiritual needs. Protestant denominations, seeing the success of Christian Endeavor, formed their own organizations for youth and prepared special curriculum materials for them. The YMCA, founded by Christian laymen in England, came to America, and it too grew rapidly. This was due in part to the YMCA's having provided housing for young single men who were attracted to the city and needed places to live.

American Society Today

Compared to a hundred years ago when industrialization was in its beginning stage, American society today is incredibly complex. Industrialization has continued, and science with its related technology has permeated almost every aspect of life, with astonishing results. Each discovery or invention seems to produce several more, so today humankind has achieved what was only dreamed about fifty years ago.

If we were to compile a list of the most important late-twentieth-century scientific and industrial developments, space exploration would probably be at the top because the results are so spectacular and because it requires the careful coordination of many technologies, especially the use of computers. High on that list would be achievements in medical science and communications, including television. Transportation was revolutionized in this century by the invention and development of the airplane. But the automobile needs to be noted too, for its invention changed how people live and the way they use time. The list could easily be lengthened, but this is enough to make the point that our scientific/technical/industrial society requires an enormous number of well-educated people to keep it going.

In addition to the education needed by the general population, professional people—especially medical doctors, lawyers, engineers, teachers, and others who are leaders in our society— require a very long period of preparation for their vocation; some professionals, such as certified public accountants, are required to take continuing education courses annually in order to maintain their certification.

Professional people have responded to the increased complexity of our society by specializing. Lawyers often specialize in tax matters or corporation affairs; doctors specialize in certain diseases or parts of the body; engineers restrict themselves to airplane design, computer manufacture, chemical manufacture, or some similar field. Specialization is a way to achieve competence in a complex society by narrowing the field of study and work. But specialization does not reduce the preparation time for professional people because they must first be doctors or engineers before they can develop specialties within those vocations.

Sometimes a major social event will mark a whole generation of teenagers. Children who came of age in the 1940s were marked for the rest of their lives by World War II. Teenagers in the 1960s who participated in the civil rights struggle have stronger beliefs about racial justice than their parents. It is too early in the 1990s to identify a major social event that may leave a lasting mark on this generation. There are, however, some social conditions that may affect their moral standards. The liberalization of attitudes about sexual activity, including that of homosexuals, the women's movement for equality, the continuing struggle of African Americans for civil rights, the development of an underclass of people who are permanently on welfare, the enlargement of the wage gap between low-paying jobs and jobs that require special training, and the resurgence of very conservative religious groups—these are some of the major movements of our time that may affect teenagers as they move into adulthood.

Society Is Interpreted by Groups

These statements about our historical eras describe general social conditions that affect almost everyone. How they affect teenagers is determined largely by the social, racial, or ethnic group to which teenagers belong. By group I mean the adults—parents, relatives, friends, and leaders—who make up the social environment to which the teenagers relate. There are many different enclaves or local communities that interpret American values their own way and communicate those interpretations to children and teenagers. One's social group converts general ideas of patriotism, equality, justice, and truth into specific patterns of conduct as the group discusses and proposes practical ways of responding to events as they happen. For this reason we must identify the social situation of the teenagers we are concerned about, for we cannot influence them unless we enter sympathetically into the communities of which they are members.

Variety of Social Groups

Francis A. J. Ianni and colleagues at Columbia University spent eighteen years studying teenagers from a number of high schools in the New York City area. In his summary of what they learned, Ianni stresses the importance of the social group to which the teenagers belong. Teenagers coming of age among low-income people on Manhattan's Lower East Side identify with the African, Chinese, or Hispanic culture of which they are a part. What they have absorbed from their group about the value of schooling, the job opportunities available to them, how to adapt to the demands of society, obedience to adults in authority such as policemen or teachers, relationships with the opposite sex, use of money, and similar matters is the basis on which they make decisions. There is a sharp contrast between these racial or ethnic teenage groups and the teenagers coming of age in predominantly white Protestant suburban villages in New Jersey, made up of mostly high-income families.[1]

What Ianni has documented from many careful studies of teenagers can be observed in general terms if one pays attention to what teenagers of a particular social group say or do. Consider, for example, children who grow up in an Old Order Amish community. They live in a rural setting that is deliberately devoid of farm machinery, electricity, and chemical fertilizers. They conclude their formal education in Amish-directed schools at an early age, for they need no further education for the kind of farming they will do. Moreover, the family has made provision for them to settle into a house on the family farm when they marry. Under these conditions teenagers will be like their parents, only younger.

Mainstreamers

We Christians who are in the mainstream of American life refer to ourselves as "middle class" and are members of well-known denominations. Although there are important differences in the social groups to which we belong, we are so much like one another in general characteristics that we can describe five essential features of our teenagers.

1. Extended period of preparation. Middle-class people expect to work in positions that require some college education. Many of our teenagers finish college. If they plan to enter a profession such as engineering, medicine, ministry, law, or business, there is an additional two to four years of education. Thus there is a period from about age twelve, the beginning of rapid physical growth, to about twenty-two to twenty-five before they enter the vocation for which they have been preparing.

This enormous extension of the period from the end of childhood to the start of an adult vocation has led psychologists to divide it into three sections. The first period, usually listed as ages ten through thirteen, is called early adolescence. This time is characterized by the trauma of getting used to a rapidly growing body and the realization that one is being pushed into more responsibility. The high school years, from ages fourteen through eighteen, are a time when most teenagers are preparing themselves for a job or for entering college. Young people from nineteen to the beginning of their vocation are often called "youth," but a more appropriate term would be "young adults." During this time they are largely on their own, although college students are often dependent on their parents for financial support. The young-adult period is very important because a lot of a person's life is consolidated during these years. However, for the purposes of this book we will focus our attention on the high school age bracket.

2. *Dependency.* Although many teenagers work for pay after school and in the summer, they live at home and are under the supervision of their parents. During early adolescence this situation causes no special problem, but toward the age of fifteen or sixteen, when most of the growth spurt is complete, tensions can arise. The basic issue is independence. Teenagers have the physical size and experience to be considered independent, and if they have a driver's license and access to a car, they have what to them is the ultimate symbol of adulthood—they can go where they want to go on their own schedule. This opens up a new world to explore, on their own or with friends. Parents who are reluctant to let go or are overly cautious about their teenager's ability to handle this freedom often put restrictions on travel or set a curfew time when the teenager must return home in the evening.

There is some evidence that any dependency situation is a possible source of hostility. If a wife or husband is dependent financially or emotionally on a spouse, the dependent one may resent the power and independence of the dominant partner. The same is true in race relations. If Native Americans feel dependent on the goodwill or generosity of white lawmakers, they may resent having to ask for what they consider to be theirs already. In a similar way teenagers, feeling that they are capable of managing their own affairs, are dependent on their parents. Except for some spending money earned in part-time jobs, teenagers do not have final decision-making power—a condition that can lead to anger directed at parents or other adults in authority.

3. *Marginal status.* Mainstream teenagers—by reason of the long period of dependency while they are preparing for a vocation in our technical/industrial society—are marginal to the actual operation of society. They lack preparation for meaningful jobs, and their labor is not needed except for work in fast-food shops or minimum-wage jobs. They are in a holding pattern. That is why their social situation is so frustrating. Most parents and interested adults want them to make good grades in school and keep out of trouble. They are told by adults to find something to do, engage in sports, try a musical instrument, work on a computer, or help with household chores—

almost any respectable thing to use up the available time while waiting to become a responsible adult. The things that would help them become responsible, such as meaningful work or participation in government, are denied them.

4. Youth culture. Given their marginal and dependent status, it is no wonder that teenagers have developed their own culture. Choosing their own music, dance, entertainment, and clothing is a way of affirming themselves and passing the time until society has a place for them. Youth culture is not something entirely apart from American culture; it is a refuge to which teenagers go as they work on their many personal problems. But this refuge is surrounded by America. Much youth culture is an exaggeration or acceleration of trends already in motion. Youth culture is an outlook they create to express their hopes, their fears, their frustrations. But it is more than imaginary. It is expressed in practical decisions about how they spend their time and money and in ideas they toss back and forth as they test themselves with one another in relation to the larger culture of which they are a part.

5. Conflict with adults. There seems always to have been a conflict between generations. The adult generation tends to look on teenagers as irresponsible troublemakers who are unwilling to settle down to a routine schedule. Here is Aristotle, writing about 2,300 years ago to describe the youth of his era:

> Young men have strong passions, and tend to gratify them indiscriminately. Of the bodily desires, it is the sexual by which they are most swayed and in which they show absence of self-control. They are changeable and fickle in their desires, which are violent while they last, but quickly over: their impulses are keen but not deep-rooted, and are like sick people's attacks of hunger and thirst. They are hot-tempered and quick-tempered, and apt to give way to their anger; bad temper often gets the better of them, for owing to their love of honour they cannot bear being slighted, and are indignant if they imagine themselves unfairly treated. . . . Their lives are mainly spent not in memory but in expectation; for expectation refers to the future, memory to the past, and youth has a long future before it and a short past behind it. . . . They have exalted notions, because they have not yet been humbled by life or learnt its necessary limitations; moreover, their hopeful disposition makes them think themselves equal to great things—and that means having exalted notions. . . . They are fond of fun and therefore witty, wit being well-bred insolence.[2]

Shakespeare, in *The Winter's Tale* (Act 3, Scene iii), expressed a similar dissatisfaction with the English youth of his time. "I would there were no age between ten and three-and-twenty, or that youth would sleep out the rest; for there is nothing in the between but getting wenches with child, wronging the ancientry, stealing, fighting."

The age-old conflict between generations was caused by youth's lack of experience. Adults thought, like Shakespeare, that young people would grow out of that stage and settle down like the older generation. To some extent the old conflict continues because some life situations do not change and young people gain wisdom as they gain experience. But a new source of conflict has arisen in American society due to inventions and discoveries.

Most scientific discoveries and technological developments affect the way we live. The tin can and the refrigerator have done as much to free women from home duties as have other forces of liberation. The development of the automobile changed the nature of our cities and freed young people to roam far beyond the confines of their homes. This generation takes the computer, space exploration, "smart" bombs, and other scientific/industrial developments in stride, but each impacts our thinking and living.

Computers, for example, are the playthings of teenagers and college students. Some young people have learned how to break into the computer systems of schools and businesses. These "hackers" have even created "viruses" by which they have "infected" computers of our major universities. Because computers were new, there were no laws or customs to control hackers and protect information. After the problem emerged, laws were passed to protect computer data, and some hackers have been tried and sentenced for breaking those laws. Most teenage hackers have strong traditional moral values, but they break into other people's computer data to test their skills. According to a computer security specialists conference held in Washington, D.C., in March 1991, teenagers have not been taught the ethics of computer behavior. The reason they have not been so instructed is because the older generation did not understand computers. In fact, the computer security specialists attending this conference could not agree among themselves on ethical standards. Some thought any unauthorized entry into computer data belonging to others was wrong. Others thought it was improper only if the hacker altered or stole information. Other conferees said adults should not make young people into criminals just because they were inquisitive and creative. After all, it was computer hackers who went on to found Apple Computer and Microsoft Corporation.[3]

Dealing with the Social Setting

The origins of a social setting are beyond our control. Historical events—such as wars, scientific discoveries, the capitalist economic system, our Christian religion, and the founding of the United States in a vast land full of natural resources—have produced the society in which we live. Unless our culture changes radically, the adolescent years will continue to be a time of preparation and dependency, a time when individuals may not vote or obtain meaningful work. We will take these conditions into account in chapter 6 when we list the practical ways a congregation can help young people develop moral standards.

We can, however, conclude this part of our study with an observation. During the teen years when growing persons are not needed by society, they have a special need to belong to a community. Recall the results of Ianni's eighteen-year study of adolescents in the New York area. He found the best way to understand this age group was to identify the social group to which they belonged. Most teenagers absorb the life-style and customs of their social group. Belonging means individuals are attached to a group of people they respect and from whom they want recognition. This basic human need for belonging to a group is compounded while waiting for adult status. If adults make the congregation a community to which people want to belong, they will be helping teenagers move more smoothly into adulthood.

CHAPTER 5

Coming of Age
—Self-Discovery

The first three chapters of this book proposed that the most effective way to help teenagers grow morally is for adults to create a community in which a Christian life-style is defined and lived. The previous chapter and this one are an interlude in which we describe the social and psychological factors that make adolescence a special stage of human development. The purpose of this interlude is to recall how young people must struggle within themselves in order to move from the dependency of childhood to the relative independence of young adulthood. After these two "coming of age" chapters, we will be ready in chapters 6 and 7 to propose practical ways a congregation may attend to the moral growth of its youth.

Teenagers come of age in a certain historical era that is interpreted to them by the social group to which they belong. But teenagers are individuals who are conscious of themselves as persons and are being pushed into adulthood. They may want to remain safe and secure within the family; but physical growth, mental development, and social expectations pressure young teenagers to become more responsible for what they do and say.

The trigger event is the combination of a rapid growth spurt with the maturation of sex organs. These developments happen within one's body on their own schedule and force one to realize that he or she is becoming an adult. The obvious physical changes, noted and discussed by family and friends, are reason enough to cause self-examination. But as teenagers become aware of their ability to create a baby, they are sobered by the power and responsibility thrust upon them without their asking. The biological urges that accompany this new physical state are strange and strong. These instincts demand attention and suggest sexual activity forbidden by society.

The result is anxiety about one's self, compounded with uncertainty and confusion about one's body.

Mental development probably produces less anxiety than do physical changes because it comes about gradually and there is no obvious sign that it is occurring. Yet teenagers are aware of their increasing ability to concentrate on their studies, to plan ahead, to understand how things work, to manipulate ideas in their mind, to imagine a different set of circumstances than those which now control their lives, to judge how other people will respond to what they say and do, and to propose solutions to everyday problems to which adults pay attention.

Social expectations mean that teenagers are becoming aware of both the hard and soft side of society. The hard side is the law, which defines the ages when they can drive, drink alcohol, and see adult movies, and when they must register for military service. They are more sensitive to the soft side of society: what their parents, relatives, and adults around them think they should be doing. Most teenagers respond positively to questions put to them by friendly adults such as "What do you plan to be?" "What school subjects do you like?" or "What do you do when you are not in school?" Constant conversation about matters of this kind to which teenagers are expected to respond with their opinions and choices is a gentle but persistent reminder of the coming day when they will be on their own.

Steps Toward Self-Discovery

Although each of these pressures on teenagers causes a certain amount of anxiety, the overriding concern of every teenager is the kind of person he or she wants to be. Teenagers know that what they are going through is not so much a stage from which they will emerge in a few years as it is a transition from childhood dependency to an adulthood in which they will have both freedom and responsibility. They know they will be different when the teen years are over, but the questions are "How different?", "In what ways different?", and "Will I like what I am becoming?"

Who Am I?

At the heart of the teenage situation is the question "Who am I?" This question is impossible to answer in a precise way, but no one can live satisfactorily without an answer that the self can respect.

The question does not arise first in the teen years; it has been thought about in later childhood. But it comes to the fore in teen years when one has to respond to physical, mental, and social pressures. Moreover, throughout young adulthood and beyond, one often goes back to the question as new conditions arise to which one has to respond.

Although the question "Who am I?" is vague and the answer uncertain, it is the question teenagers ask as they face practical problems and choices. When they are in a position to cheat or are pressed by peers to steal something just to see if they can get away with it, the question comes to the fore: "Am I that kind of person?" The same is true when they are in a position to go beyond ordinary boundaries in sexual experimentation or in using drugs. The question also summarizes their dilemma when the opportunity is given to play a musical instrument, to go out for an athletic team, to become a cheerleader, or to start a hobby. When new opportunities open up, the question returns: "Does that represent something I am really interested in?"

Erik Erikson introduced the term "ego identity" as descriptive of this adolescent stage. Although there are wide differences in the age when it comes into consciousness, the high school age bracket is most likely the time when teenagers become aware of their struggle to find themselves. In typical cases teenagers go through a time of confusion, when the internal attitudes and values they acquired in childhood are questioned and they seem not to be able to commit themselves to any particular outlook, vocational goal, or moral standard. Then comes a time of testing, when they consider different ideas of what they want to be and what they want to accomplish. This reflection and brooding may take place in a "moratorium" state, which could be a time away from home. Some young people may relieve their inner tension by a "foreclosure" in which they accept a set of beliefs, vocational goals, or style of life because it is presented to them in a winsome way or by an adult they admire. This is a premature answer to the question "Who am I?" Teenagers who work their way slowly through the identity issue will come to a set of commitments about their vocation and the kind of person they want to be and will acknowledge values by which they want to live. Erikson calls this "identity achievement."[1]

A self-identity that teenagers like and enjoy explaining to parents and friends is achieved—according to Erikson—in three areas: time, work, and relations with other people. In Erikson's analysis, when young people face a situation or crisis, one can tell by their behavior whether they are meeting that situation constructively and are therefore becoming more mature or whether they are unable to respond properly. In relation to time one can see whether teenagers are beginning to take charge of the time that is available and how they allocate it to different tasks. Taking responsibility for waking up in the morning and getting ready for school is a good indicator. Teenagers need lots of support and help to set and keep a schedule, but this is something they know how to do and they recognize its importance. A poor response is made when teenagers lose a time perspective. They then retreat inwardly to early childhood, when the time schedule was informal, and they resist adult efforts to maintain a more rigorous schedule. Since time is something over which they have some control, teenagers sometimes use it to show resistance to adult authority.

Work is another area in which young people must find themselves. Even if one is working only for pay or because it is a duty to the family, there is gratification in doing the job right. This gratification has to do with the way one sees one's self, not necessarily with the significance of the job itself, for doing a job that needs to be done and doing it well is something that counts in the adult world. However, if teenagers have an opportunity to work as apprentices in jobs where judgment, skill, understanding, knowledge, and experience are acquired, and if the job has some positive social values, the work can also serve as a test of their vocational interest. Thus working in a hospital, automobile shop, newspaper, or library might clarify vocational goals. If teenagers' work experiences do not go well, they feel inadequate, lose concentration, and spend too much time on unimportant things. Or they jump from one thing to another without much effort to understand what each project is about.

Teenagers also work on the "Who am I?" question in relation to other people, especially adults. They do this by careful observation of the adults with whom they have close association. They may form a psychological kinship with a few adults who represent what they want to be. This does not mean that teenagers are in close contact with the adults on whom they have a crush. The person with whom they identify could be a teacher, coach, singer, community leader, or minister whom they see in all kinds of situations, even though it may be at a distance. However, at the deepest level of their being, many adolescents lock on to an adult who embodies what they want to be. Although the crush is personal and often secret, teenagers may imitate the speech, dress, gestures, or other overt characteristics of the adults they admire.

This identification of one's self with others and looking to those persons for inspiration and, perhaps, guidance is not unique to the teen years. Children form similar associations with adults with whom they are close, and even adults constantly relate to others who embody their values. The difference in the teen years is in the use that is made of the relationship. Teenagers are questioning or dissolving some of the ideas of who they are that they had absorbed from parents and neighbors. They have not yet become conscious of who they are and exactly what they want to be. During this period, teenagers are unusually alert to adults who seem to be what they want to be. Their relationship to these adults is intense even though the adults may be unaware of their influence. Teenagers use this model of the kind of life they want as they slowly adopt or adapt what they see in adults they admire. When they have bridged the gap and are sure of who they are, their need for an internal psychological relationship with adults lessens, but they will probably carry throughout their life a special fondness for the adults who unwittingly helped them discover their real selves.

This process of identification with adults can sometimes be negative, rather than positive. A boy may have a strong identification with his father, including the father's alcoholism. The son may know that drinking alcohol is bad for his health but drinks because his father does. Some young people feel they cannot live up to the ideals or ambitions of their parents, so they engage in antisocial or dangerous behavior in order to have something they can call their own.[2]

Help

As teenagers struggle to discover themselves, they learn they are not alone in the enterprise; others have been through the same period of transition. These older people offer hints and suggestions. In a more formal way young people are helped in their identity formation by (1) their family, (2) the school and agencies of government, (3) the church and community organizations, (4) their peer groups. Each of these four sources of help is so different that we can do no more than note their importance and role.

1. The family. Teenagers usually live in some kind of family situation, although each family is different. Modern society does not provide much support for the family. Employment demands often keep one of the parents, usually the father, out of the home most of the week, and changing employment may require frequent moving. In a high percentage of families, both parents work outside the home. Also, the number of single parents has increased dramatically during the past few decades. Thus, teenagers today are often on their own after school and in the summer. However, being at home even with little time for conversation with parents provides a sense of belonging and stability, with the possibility of some guidance, while teenagers are seeking the selves they want to be.

2. Schools and government agencies. Most public high schools today are huge, complex organizations, managed by several layers of administrators and served by specialists in addition to teachers. Students do not expect and seldom receive very much personal attention. Yet the high school helps teenagers define themselves. This is done partly in the academic realm, where students—for the first time in their formal education career—have an opportunity to select some courses according to interest; it is done partly in the freedom of the schedule, for students can often choose activities, especially clubs and interest groups; it is done partly in the style of education, for students are given more responsibility to work on their own schedules and do projects of their own selection; it is done in athletics, where a wide range of sports is available, with coaches to help develop their abilities. In addition, many high schools have a counseling service where a student can go for vocational testing and guidance.

Governmental agencies, by reason of their size and impersonal nature, cannot do much to help individuals with their inner struggles. They can, however, be significant. Police, for example, are the representatives of government teenagers do see and often deal with. If the police are fair and just in their treatment of a teenager regardless of race, gender, clothing, or hairstyle, the teenager may learn to respect law and government.

3. Church and community organizations. About half of all teenagers belong to a YMCA, a Girl or Boy Scout troop, or a similar community organization. These youth-serving agencies provide quite an array of activities. Teenagers can find places where they are wanted and where their needs are served.

About 86 percent of high schoolers report they are being raised in a religious tradition. How many are enrolled in church programs is difficult to determine, but most of this 86 percent are related to organized religious groups. The problem of teenagers in mainstream Protestant denominations is the gradual decline in their attendance during high school years and their disappearance from churches after graduation.[3]

4. Peer groups. Friends one's own age are important throughout life. Children learn to share, to control their aggressive behavior, to play for fun, and to recognize themselves as important persons in birthday parties and other matters of human relations through their peer groups. Adults cluster in groups according to interest or vocation, and they form support groups to help each other with problems such as alcoholism, weight loss, or the trauma of a deadly disease.

During the teen years, peer groups are of critical importance. The decisive changes that take place in the bodies, minds, and social relations of adolescents create a state of anxiety, and they increasingly turn to peers who are going through the same adjustment. Although parents can be helpful, they are often part of the problem because parents still control the teenagers' living arrangements, spending money, and use of a car and are held legally responsible for the teenagers' actions. Adolescents are too baffled by all the pressures from within and the requirements from without to understand clearly that they are involved in a delicate psychological task. They are trying to become more independent, more self-sufficient, while still in the family setting where parents usually see them as dependent children. About the only place they can turn for sympathy, support, and strategies for dealing with parents is to their peers. Thus the peer group is for a time a substitute for the family, the place where they can talk freely while they are forming new relationships with their parents and with adults in authority.

Peer groups change with age. Early adolescents, ten through thirteen years of age, are expanding beyond the neighborhood play group into a larger social arena. They are granted more freedom because they can take care of themselves and have a lively interest in the world about them. This is the time when they join the Girl Scouts or Boy Scouts, or, if they are in a 4-H club, they take responsibility for the care of animals they exhibit in county fairs. Because these years are the beginning of sexual maturation, individuals feel more comfortable with others of their own gender. If there is a time when people should be grouped by sex, this is that time.

Middle adolescence, ages fourteen through eighteen, is the time when peer groups are most meaningful. During this period teenagers have become somewhat accustomed to their physical growth and are more concerned to use their rapidly expanded mental powers to make sense out of the new world into which they are moving. They associate with large groups having similar interests or background. On a high school campus just before the beginning of the school day, one can see loosely formed groups of students gathered by racial, ethnic, social, or special interests milling about. Some large organized groups are athletic teams, choirs, hobby clubs, and drama or church groups. These large coeducational groups are often called crowds. They provide various ways for teenagers to congregate, including parties. From this pool of people, individuals seek and find friends for a small group to which they can become deeply attached.

The small group, often called a clique, or gang, is sometimes made up of members of the same sex. If it is a same-sex gang, they are interested in the opposite sex as well as in their own personal problems. Cliques or gangs are small, seldom more than seven or eight in number. Because these small groups are so intense about themselves, they are made up of young people who are about the same age, race, and family status in the community. The homogeneous nature of small groups may be criticized from an ideological or religious viewpoint, but, as they form their self-image, teenagers need the security of having like-minded friends while they deal with the passions within and the pressures from without.

A small group or clique is bonded by mutual affection. The group may not see one another as a group on a regular schedule, but the members constantly talk back and forth, usually by phone. The length of time on the phone is often a point of conflict with parents. Teenagers, however, are not so much listening to one another as they are talking to themselves about their problems while a friend listens and responds. This need for like-minded persons to respond has produced a peer counseling plan whereby two teenagers agree to talk to each other for a period of time, usually one hour equally divided. This procedure seems to be all that is needed for many teenagers to work through their frustrations, hopes, and fears.

Friendships that develop during the high school years are often recalled by adults as the best they ever had. This does not mean that friends keep in close touch with each other after high school; it does mean that, during that time of change when one needed a peer to take the place of a parent, there was one who listened and responded. Because the friend came along at a critical time of need, one remembers that person with special fondness, long after the need has been met and one moves on to other things.

The implication of this description of peer groups is that the experience is positive and helps teenagers move to clearer conceptions of themselves. For many, perhaps most, that is the case. But it is not the situation for some others. The peer group is a personal and social experience with considerable power. *What* that experience is like depends on the group. Because of their insecurity, teenagers are vulnerable to peer pressure to conform to what the group thinks is good behavior. What is good (exciting, cool, or adventuresome) for some groups could be drinking alcohol, experimenting with drugs or sexual activity, stealing, or other forms of delinquency. Moreover, peer group members, by their constant talking about people and events, can be the source or intensification of prejudice against racial or ethnic groups or any group that does not conform to their idea of what is good and right. The need for a peer group is so great among adolescents that they will often say or do whatever the group desires in order not to be rejected.

Continuity and Change

The period from age twelve through sixteen, or to graduation from high school, is marked by both continuity and change. Persons moving through these years consider themselves to be the same because the traits that make up their character remain fairly consistent. Their interests, spirit of pessimism or optimism, ambitions, values, sympathy for people less fortunate, concern for the rights of others, openness to new ideas, approach to problem-solving, and similar traits continue throughout this period.[4]

Teenagers' ability to discuss and express these traits or personal preferences improves during this period because their minds are becoming more mature, but their underlying character does not change very much. Some teenagers may change a basic characteristic, but that usually happens only if a traumatic experience forces them to alter their outlook. Most teenagers use their developing mental powers to review and perhaps revise somewhat the character traits they already have.

What does change during these four to six years is a person's mental ability. Joseph Adelson and associates found in their studies of over a thousand adolescents ages eleven to eighteen that it is sheer maturation of the person during this time, rather than race, gender, social class, or level of intelligence, which accounts for the increasing complexity of their thought processes. The average twelve-year-old cannot explain what a political party is, but by age eighteen he or she can give a rather sensible account of what political parties are and how they function. Adelson found a childish understanding of morality at age twelve: That is, things are right or wrong and people who do wrong things should be punished. Later, after their thinking had matured, teenagers were able to consider why criminals act the way they do and to understand that circumstances in a case can change what one thinks about the crime and, to some extent, what effect jail or other punishment might have on people who break laws.[5] The difference in mental ability between the ages of twelve and eighteen is enormous, not just in one's ability to think logically but in the ability to make judgments, the highest level of mental activity. And it is not just the capacity to understand that circumstances alter cases of crime; it is the ability to apply general values to concrete situations, the highest level of moral reasoning.[6]

We must be careful not to draw false conclusions from the profound development of the mind during the teen years. It does not mean that all or even most teenagers will exercise the mental ability that is now in place. Although they can make judgments based on facts and reason, many will not do so. This may come about because there is little stimulation (for wealthy, coddled teenagers) or because there is a feeling that such mental work has no reward (for poor teenagers). Others may be dimly aware that they are now adult in mental ability but do not care about that part of their self because they are busy with other interests.

Nor does it mean that because teenagers have the capacity to relate complex life experiences to values, the values they have will be modified by reason. American culture contains the idealistic notion that there is a good, happy state of human affairs toward which individuals and the government should aim and that, as their thinking matures, people will be guided by reason to make justice the highest moral value. This basic assumption shows up in some moralists who have constructed a stair-step set of stages through which people go as their mental processes become more mature. Adelson found some evidence for this idealism in his interview with teenagers. As they grew older, teenagers in America and in several Western nations shifted away from simple authoritarian views of law and order to a more complex understanding of individual rights, long-term concerns of society, and the differences between goals and the means of reaching those goals. By late adolescence it was found that teenagers had become more "liberal, humane, and democratic."[7] But one cannot say that the development of the mind caused this trend. It is more likely a result of personal acceptance and comprehension of the culture in which they were coming of age. In fact teenagers, when asked about the possibility of eliminating crime, poverty, and racial prejudice, became increasingly pessimistic as they grew older. Likewise, eighteen-year-olds were more cynical about the influence of "important" people in society than were the twelve-year-olds.[8]

Thus, teenagers may—because of their maturing minds—become more accepting of the values that underlie American society and at the same time more realistic about the power of society to corrupt individuals. So the development of the mind's ability to reason does not carry with it any moral standards or beliefs. If a teenage boy is a member of a street gang that extorts lunch money from younger children and robs older people sitting in parks, it is more likely that, as his reasoning ability matures, he will become more efficient as a thief rather than that his reasoning will cause him to become honest.

CHAPTER 6

Helping Teenagers
—Involvement

We have described the congregation as being a community with the possibility of exerting a powerful influence on the morals of youth. We have looked at the adolescent years as a period when individuals are developing the selves they want and for which they are responsible. In this and the next chapter we will discuss practical ways adults in a congregation can help young people grow morally.

Through its influence with parents, the church may be a significant factor in the moral development of children and youth at every age. However, there are two periods of enormous physical, mental, and moral development to which we must give special attention. The first is from the period of birth to about age four or five. Babies are helpless, having only the instinct to survive and grow, but by age three they have matured to the place where they can feed themselves, put on their clothes, carry on a conversation in which they express their likes and dislikes, show affection, play with other children, and adhere to a daily schedule. During their first four or five years children also develop a conscience, which motivates their behavior in profound ways. They learn to feel guilty when they do forbidden things for which they are punished. They experience shame when they fail to live up to the expectations of their parents or the care-giving adults in their home. During this first period of enormous physical growth and development of selfhood, the church's influence in religious moral training is primarily through parents and care-giving adults and secondarily in day-care centers and Sunday school classes.

The Adolescent Years

The second period of rapid growth is during the years from about age twelve through sixteen. We discussed this period in chapters 4 and 5 under the theme Coming of Age. We can summarize the importance of the adolescent years for moral growth by noting that during this time individuals are testing both their beliefs and the moral standards of their childhood.

As teenagers develop their ability to think abstractly and to understand how historical events have shaped their lives, they examine the beliefs by which they have been living. This examination includes—but is not limited to—religious beliefs. Young people question themselves and one another about beliefs they hear expressed, such as: can war settle international disputes, are certain races superior to other races, are sexual relations between consenting people OK, is college education necessary for a good life, and will having money make one happy? Since morals are based on one's beliefs, it is extremely important for the church to influence teenagers' thinking during this critical period.

As teenagers gain more freedom to work and play beyond the home and neighborhood and comprehend different life-styles from television and movies, they cannot help but question the conventional moral standards they absorbed in childhood. Those moral standards were imposed on them by parental authority when they were very young and by persuasion as they grew older. Now, during the teen years, they realize they are becoming free to decide things for themselves and have more opportunity to do so away from their parents. Seldom do young people make a sudden radical break with their moral code. Rather, they test it in conversation with peers and family and often test it in action. A common area of testing is stealing. Teenagers know it is wrong to steal, and most live by that standard. But when they get together in gangs in a shopping mall, they often shoplift for the thrill of it; they are testing the boundaries of society as, when small children, they tested how far they could go in taking things they wanted before their parents stopped them.

This inclination to test one's beliefs and test one's childhood moral standards presents parents and other adults with a serious dilemma. We want our youth to exercise their newly acquired ability to reason abstractly so they will become independent thinkers. But we are afraid that their inexperience in human affairs will lead them into radical beliefs. If young people do not test their morals, their morals will never be their own. On the one hand, they may live good lives by conventional morals, but they will be childlike in obeying an external authority rather than acting out of their own inner convictions. On the other hand, when young people test their conventional morals, they may hurt someone or make mistakes they will regret for years to come.

This dilemma is a condition we must work with and monitor in order to supply whatever is needed to help youngsters evaluate their morals. The problem is how to do so. Parents are important, but parents are also part of the dilemma, for the teenagers are also testing their parents' beliefs and morals. Thus young people turn to peers and to other adults for help as they evaluate the moral standards they see in operation. If peers and adults are in a congregation, teenagers may receive constructive guidance and the stabilizing influence of a community of concerned people.

Four Ways to Be Involved

The question of how to help young people grow morally has many answers. Moreover, there may be some truth in each. So the problem is to identify the most effective methods and give them highest priority. Otherwise, we will spend too much time and energy on procedures that do not produce lasting results. In this chapter we will discuss, in priority order, four methods of moral education that emphasize involvement. In the next chapter we will discuss four methods, also in priority order, that feature discussion. Of course, involvement and discussion overlap in each group of methods, but it is important to understand that, in terms of moral education, involvement in a community is a more powerful method than discussion.

1. Be An Actively Involved Community

The civil rights movement and the Mormon church were used in chapter 1 to illustrate the involvement principle. Adults in black congregations during the 1950s and 1960s did not plan a program to instruct their youth about racial injustice. Adults influenced their congregations to be a community where racial injustice was a major concern expressed in sermons, songs, prayers, reports of unjust treatment, celebrations over events that marked progress, and so on. Teenagers who belonged to such a congregation were influenced to become involved in the movement, and when they participated they were encouraged and supported by the congregation.

The Mormon church presents a different situation. Congregations of this religion have well-defined beliefs and morals that shape their communal life. Their communal life, in turn, forms the religious life of its members. The Mormon church is not engaged in some dramatic and intense struggle with society about a specific issue, as the black church was about race relations. But the Mormon church knows itself as having beliefs and morals different from the society in which it is located, so its congregations embody those differences.

The primacy of involvement as an educational principle is best illustrated by the way we learn a language. The easiest and most effective way to learn a language is to live in a community where that language is spoken. If you wanted to understand the language better, you would learn to write it and then you would read literature and history from communities in which that language was used.

The most important contribution a congregation can make to the ethical growth of teenagers is to be a community where people care for one another and are deeply concerned to practice the Christian faith. The worship and work of such a congregation will shape the lives of adults, including parents, with whom the teenagers relate. The way adults act and speak because of their faith in God is probably the most influential factor in moral development.

Does involvement in congregational life mean that morals are "caught" from people around us rather than "taught"? The answer is no, for both go on simultaneously. One of the characteristics of moral action is that we almost always explain to ourselves or to others why we decided an issue a certain way. This is because morals are something we consider in our own mind and also with other people as we weigh the pros and cons of our actions.

Teenagers go through the same process in their minds and with their peers. They need and often seek adults—other than their parents—who will talk with them about their moral problems and the results of various solutions. Adults in small congregations where everyone knows everyone can be of significant help to the moral growth of young people if they will converse with them in a friendly way. In such an environment teenagers can test their beliefs and morals with adults who are interested in them but have no authority over them.

In large congregations some organized effort is necessary to provide occasions when adults and young people can meet and talk in an informal manner. One large congregation invites everyone to participate in an Extended Family program. Each extended family is limited to about fifteen people including family units, single adults, college students, and children of all ages. This extended family meets in homes on a regular schedule and celebrates birthdays, awards, and the like. It also considers prayerfully the illnesses, accidents, and hard times that members are experiencing. Adults in such a grouping have many opportunities to talk informally with young people about the way they are interpreting events in their lives and the basis on which they are making decisions.

The normal time for people to become full members of the church is during their teen years. Most congregations have confirmation or church membership classes to explain the meaning of membership and to define the meaning of a Christian way of life. Some churches are now appointing an adult sponsor for each teenager in the confirmation class. The purpose is to provide an adult who will relate to the youth as a friend. This arrangement gives adults an opportunity to enter informally into the lives of young people, share their hopes and plans for the future, and build the communal aspects of church membership. The use of sponsors in the confirmation process demonstrates that Christianity involves caring for one another as well as knowing what we believe.

2. Provide Help for Parents and Adult Leaders

The relation of teenagers to their parents has been traditionally interpreted as a time of tension, disruption, and rebellion. The findings from research done since the 1970s indicate that families experiencing such difficulties usually have had a history of problems before the child entered adolescence. The accumulated evidence from many different studies of thousands of teenagers shows that most teenagers get along rather well with their parents and share many of their parents' values. As a result, students of adolescent development are using terms such as "transformation" or "realignment" to characterize the process of adaptation that takes place when teenagers become old enough to be somewhat independent from their parents yet are still living at home.[1]

There are conflicts between young teenagers and parents, but most differences of opinion are about matters of dress, hairstyle, or doing assigned household duties. Older teenagers and their parents disagree about dating, curfew hours, drinking alcohol, doing school assignments, or using the family car. In spite of these differences, teenagers usually are positive about their parents. In a national survey of high school students, over 70 percent of teenagers said their ideas about education, religion, and values were "very similar" or "mostly similar" to those of their parents.[2]

A survey of students in the fifth through ninth grades and their parents who were members of churches produced similar results. Sixty-six percent of these young adolescents reported their relationships with their parents as very good or excellent and 20 percent rated the relationship as good. This study summarizes an enormous amount of data as follows:

> On the whole, we see parents who are genuinely struggling to be good parents, young adolescents who feel relatively good about their parent or parents, parent-child relationships which are much more affectionate and supportive than rejecting or hostile, parents and children who like to be with each other, and families relatively immune to major crises such as chemical dependency, abuse, or violence.[3]

By carefully correlating data from the teenagers' questionnaires with data from their parents', the researchers were able to generalize that parents "are significant role models for their youth, for better or worse."[4]

A recent national survey reports that 95 percent of this nation's sample of young people have parents who care what happens to them, and 64 percent would turn to their parents for moral advice. As the researchers summarized this part of their survey: "Adults have a decisive influence in the lives of children, not simply because of their formal teaching, but also in the examples they set and experiences they share."[5] This study also notes that adults in the community—religious leaders, school counselors, leaders of youth organizations, entertainers, and athletes—influence the moral choices of teenagers.

This positive relation between most teenagers and their parents means there is enough mutual respect to form the basis for a constructive dialogue about moral issues. Parents, however, often need help in understanding the need of their teenagers for freedom, the limits of freedom, how to give rewards and punishments in relation to rules, and what to do if teenagers go too far in their rebellion against restraints. Teenagers are trying to find and justify their own moral standards from among the different behavior patterns they see displayed in the lives of other teenagers and adults. Parents, being closest to the teenagers and knowledgeable about their whole life situation, are in a position to be the most influential persons during these years.

The role of the congregation is to help parents with this opportunity to influence the moral choices of teenagers. One way would be to have a class for parents of teenagers. The group could have as its religious study the same material that the teenagers were using. This would make it possible for the parents to talk with their teenagers about the material they were discussing in church school. Parents could also allocate time in their class for discussion of the specific moral problems they face with their teenagers. For this part of their group time, they might want to invite someone in the community who works with teenagers to lead their discussion. People with this kind of experience would include social workers, psychologists, professors of education, counselors, and certain high school teachers.

Most teenagers do not have an opportunity to know many adults except for relatives, neighbors, or work supervisors. Congregations, however, provide opportunities for teenagers to know many other adults. In chapter 3 it was suggested that teenagers serve as members of church committees in order to help them understand and appreciate the moral and religious assumptions that go into decision-making. Such a process would also provide occasions whereby teenagers would identify with adults while engaged in important work. Other opportunities could be created once we see adults *as a resource* for the spiritual life of teenagers. For example, a plan could be worked out whereby teenagers interview adults on a one-to-one basis. The teenagers would need some help in working out topics to discuss, and the adults should be informed of these topics. Teenagers might consider questions such as the following: What kind of moral problems do you (the adult) face in your work, and how do you deal with them? How does your religious faith help you in moral decision-making? Should the congregation sponsor forums on moral issues in order to help members think through the issues from a Christian perspective? What do you consider to be the two major moral problems in the community? Why? What can Christians do about these two problems? After the one-on-one conversation, it would be very important for the teenagers to meet as a group to share what they have heard and to formulate their answers to the questions they posed to the adults.

3. Support a Church Youth Group

Close behind the influence of parents and adults is the peer group, which for many teenagers is a temporary substitute for the family. The peer group consists of friends who will listen, understand, make suggestions, and support a teenager struggling with a moral dilemma. Because the peer group is accepting and nonjudgmental, teenagers are free to be themselves as they test different ways to respond to the situations they face. Many peer groups go beyond talking to test their emerging ideas of what is right and wrong in real life. Probably the most profound and longest-lasting moral education of teenagers takes place in peer groups when the group acts on its assumptions and from that experience forms its own moral assumptions. This applies equally to teenage gangs stealing cars or to youth groups volunteering to help build houses for poor people.

Teenagers will join or form groups because they need support from peers as they shift from the restraints of childhood to the more independent status of adulthood. Part of their struggle is to redefine themselves in relation to their parents and in the realm of what is considered right and wrong conduct. During this time teenagers are attentive to the moral standards of their peer groups while they formulate a code of right and wrong for themselves.

It is for this reason that peer groups as such, regardless of purpose, have a tremendous influence on the moral development of teenagers. Church youth groups such as a choir, sports team, Sunday school class, or study group can be very significant. In church groups teenagers have opportunities to construct their own world, try out leadership roles, gain recognition from families, and relate to adult leaders who model the moral standards of the church. Teenagers in groups engage in a dynamic interchange of ideas, constantly positioning themselves in relation to events that are important and testing their opinions with their peers. This dialogical process is at the heart of ethics, for an ethical position is one that a person has thought about, is able to explain, and can offer reasons why it is right. Adults, therefore, should respect a teenager's peer group as an area where moral standards are uppermost.

Given the ambivalence and anxiety of teenagers during this formative period, church youth groups need the best adult leaders the congregation can provide. The most important quality of adult leaders is Christian character. Much of the work of a church youth group is done informally, and most of the influence of the adult leader takes place in conversations with individuals. What the adult leaders are, therefore, shines through all they do. Teenagers are more sensitive to examples of how adults live by their faith than they are to abstract doctrinal statements. A married couple (age not too important) may be the best form of leadership the congregation can offer, for the teenagers would have before them, in addition to other Christian qualities, an example of what the church regards as the proper relationship of the sexes.

Adults should realize that many youth leaders think the youth group is not supported by the whole congregation. This comes about because teenagers, as pointed out in the section called "Mainstreamers" in chapter 4, are considered by adults to be in a holding pattern. Middle-class young people are perceived to be in training for a vocation or profession that requires years of preparation. During this training time, adults want adolescents to do well in school and keep out of trouble. They are not expected to contribute much in terms of work or wisdom to the family, church, or community.

This view of teenagers as living in a holding pattern until they become young adults may cause church officers to misjudge their relationship to the youth group. One misjudgment is to give the youth group too much, on the theory that adults can show their concern and support with gifts. This may take the form of providing a specially designed place to meet, supplying catered meals, or funding vacation-type trips. Church officers should confer with youth leaders and some representative young people about ways the youth group fits into the financial and organizational structure of the congregation. This should lead to shared responsibility, which may be expressed in supplying food if the young people will prepare it and clean up afterward. If a trip is planned, the officers may supply some money if the teenagers will use some of their own money and earn the rest through car washes or other work projects.

Another misjudgment is to assume that teenagers cannot contribute very much to the life and work of the congregation. There are many things teenagers can do on a regular basis to help with the ongoing life of a congregation. They can do some forms of office work, do certain maintenance and repair work on the buildings and grounds, and help with public worship by reading scripture and ushering. The point is not to make work but to find work that needs to be done that fits the abilities of young people. The reason is not to keep them busy so they will not get into trouble but to help them learn what is needed for a congregation to be a community of God's people. When such work is done or participation in congregational affairs is arranged, the teenagers should receive the same kind of notice or acknowledgment the adults receive.

4. Encourage Significant Projects

A church youth group engaged in significant projects has a greater potential for speeding up the thought processes leading to a Christian understanding of ethics than a group that is self-centered. This is because a "significant" project is a unit of work that is good in itself, that needs to be done, and that has value for the people involved. Why the project needs to be done and the values involved must be discussed in order to establish the ethical position.

Most communities offer teenagers opportunities to serve or work in nonprofit organizations. Some hospitals enlist high school students for patient services. Church groups often sponsor tutoring programs in which teenagers can serve. Many communities have a unit of Habitat for Humanity, an organization that builds low-cost housing. The labor for Habitat for Humanity is volunteer, and much of the work can be done by unskilled people. Building a house is a good project, because a team of teenagers could work on Saturdays along with adults. Construction of this type is rewarding; in future years these same young people may drive by the house and feel again the satisfaction of knowing that their work contributed to the well-being of a family who needed help.

Finding or creating significant projects is normally an adult responsibility, since teenagers are not experienced enough to understand all the conditions involved. Projects that involve travel, for example, require special insurance; a project abroad may require advance medical precautions. The role of an adult is that of a facilitator, someone who can anticipate what is needed to make the project a learning experience.

There is an extremely important but subtle distinction between "service" projects undertaken because Christians "ought" to serve and projects designed for ethical education. Service to others was one of the distinctive teachings of Jesus and was identified as a virtue in the New Testament church. It is one of the most universally understood values of the church today and is a strong motive, even for individuals who have dropped out of congregational life. This general motive of service to others will probably be a part of the religious makeup of teenagers and will provide the basis for launching a significant project. But adult leaders of youth groups should see that, in teaching ethics, more is involved than "service."

In order to help teenagers become ethical in our secular society, projects should be designed to help teenagers understand both the society in which they find themselves and the way the Christian faith criticizes and relates to that society. In practical terms adults should keep three things uppermost in their minds as they proceed. (1) Unless teenagers are exposed to—and have experience with— some segment of society or some culture other than their own, they will probably not be able to understand the moral assumptions that have shaped their lives. Projects outside their normal circle of friends will help bring this awareness to consciousness, where it can be discussed and compared to the Christian faith. (2) Unless teenagers participate in real situations where talk and actions have an immediate impact on other people, they will probably not understand the moral assumptions by which other people live. Projects in which they have to take some responsibility for what they say and how they act will give teenagers practice in separating the real world in which people live from fantasies or unrealistic expectations they have of other people. (3) Unless teenagers discuss what ought to be or happen in situations in which they have been involved, they will probably not move from their childhood religion to a mature faith.

These three principles are most obviously at work when a teenage group becomes involved with people in another country or section of the United States. But such projects require considerable planning and are too expensive for most youth groups. However, in every community there are usually human situations related to people from different racial/ethnic or social backgrounds that provide opportunity for ethical reflection. Hunger and homelessness, for example, are complex situations with many causes and few solutions. If adult leaders and teenagers agreed that these are important matters to explore, there would be many facets to investigate. One would be the volunteers who manage the local food bank. Why do they give their time? What is the role of compassion and concern for others in society? Why did "care for others" come out of the Jewish and Christian religions and not from Greek ethics? Another facet would be to participate in some phase of support for the local food bank by holding a car wash or a door-to-door collection of food. Another but more complex facet would be for teenagers to talk with some homeless people about their situation or to interview local people who work with homeless people in order to gain some first-hand data about why these people have no place to live.

CHAPTER 7

Helping Teenagers
—Discussion

The four strategies for moral education discussed in chapter 6 "involved" people in moral issues or projects. Involvement created discussion, and the discussion influenced the way individuals participated in communal activities. Those four methods of involvement are our most dynamic ways of helping teenagers grow morally.

The four strategies discussed in this chapter are also important and useful. They are less effective than the first four because they do not require a person to do anything. This appraisal of effectiveness in moral education comes from research done in public schools. Public schools in recent years have become more concerned about moral education, and curricula have been developed for classroom use. The Association for Supervision and Curriculum Development (ASCD) appointed a distinguished panel of researchers and educators to report on the present status of these programs. This panel first noted there were two widely known curricula for moral education. One used the cognitive-development theory of Lawrence Kohlberg, and the other used the values-clarification approach developed by Louis Raths and associates. Both curricula centered on an individual's thinking about a moral dilemma or a moral problem. The basic idea was that, if youngsters were trained to think about moral situations and discuss their ideas with peers and teachers, they would apply their reasoned conclusions to real life situations. There has been considerable research on the effectiveness of these two approaches, which use reasoning and discussion as the primary way to help youngsters become morally mature. Research shows that the cognitive-development method has some effect on reasoning, but values clarification has none. Neither of these two widely used methods of moral education has been able to demonstrate that it influences students' behavior when they make their own moral choices. The panel of researchers who studied this matter suggested that, if the two approaches were used within a community, they might be more successful.[1]

This suggestion is our clue as to how reasoning and discussion methods may be effective. If we use such methods in a church class-room as part of a caring community, they may be extremely helpful. Moreover, if discussion methods lead people to think about moral issues, they may change their morals or become engaged in a moral issue. So discussion as a method is important. It is also an easy way to begin, for almost everyone has an opinion on moral matters and is willing to discuss it. Let us now consider four methods that start with discussion.

1. Foster Discussions of Teenagers' Moral Situations

Discussion of teenagers' moral situations are important because such problems are the ones they must solve. Moral problems, as teenagers see them, are often in the realm of personality and are not easily turned into issues that affect other people. The Search Insti-tute survey of church youth revealed that the top four interests of teenagers were "learning how to make friends and be a friend," "finding out what is special about me," "figuring out what it means to be a Christian," and "learning about what is right and wrong."[2] This cluster of interests illustrates teenagers' preoccupation with themselves, but the last two could become an entry point for a dis-cussion of the moral situations they face and the basis on which they should respond. The Harris survey of teenagers asked this question: "Of these problems facing kids today, which one do you worry about most for yourself?" The top four answers were "pressure to do well in school or sports," "what to do with your life," "drug us-age," and "lack of close friends."[3] This cluster of questions is like-wise self-centered, but it reveals the areas teenagers are motivated to explore.

The Harris survey assumed that moral standards are abstractions or generalizations that are often violated. The researchers therefore described a series of life situations and asked the teenagers to indi-cate how they would respond. Forty-seven percent said they would cheat on a test, 5 percent would take money from parents without their permission, 36 percent would not tell the truth to the school principal about a friend who destroyed school property, 25 percent would drink alcohol at a party even though it is illegal, and 60 percent would be willing on a third date to go beyond kissing with a person they liked. Abortion is such a public issue and is so close to the experience of teenagers that we should note the advice they would give to an unmarried pregnant friend. Only 12 percent would advise abortion, 21 percent would advise having the baby and giving it up for adoption, 36 percent would advise keeping the baby, and 32 percent said they did not have an opinion. When asked who should make the final decision, 70 percent said the girl should and 13 percent said her parents should.[4]

These data from the Harris survey showed variations in answers according to the child's gender, race, family income, religion, and age. Children who used religious assumptions as a basis for moral decisions reported less cheating, less lying, less underage drinking of alcohol, and were less liberal in their sexual behavior. But as teenagers advanced in age, even the religious ones were more likely to cheat, lie, drink under age, and become more liberal in their sexual attitude.[5] Although no explanation is offered for this gradual shift in behavior, it probably happens because the influence of home and church grows weaker and the influence of secular society is stronger as teenagers become older.

Adult leaders of youth groups have two opportunities for helping teenagers work through the moral situations about which they must make decisions. One is conversation. Talking to a teenager one on one is an effective way to get a situation out in the open where the teenager can see it more objectively and deal with it more rationally. Helping a teenager think through options is a form of guidance any interested adult can do. The other opportunity is group discussion. The discussion could be set up with a few teenagers to help select the situations about which they want help. Or the adult leader could select newspaper stories of cheating, lying, sexual misconduct, or alcohol and drug abuse as a way of opening up a consideration of how Christians should act.

Many of the personal moral issues mentioned about which young people must make decisions are issues for adults also. In fact, much of what teenagers know about these issues comes from adults they see on television or read about in the newspapers. It would be desirable if a congregation could sponsor some adult discussions of these and related topics and invite the teenagers to participate. Care must be taken to see that the young people are allowed to speak. Their questions or observations must be respected as much as those of the adults in the meeting. The reason for such a joint meeting is to help create a feeling that Christians, regardless of age, should respond in a distinctive way to these matters and should support one another in an effort to live by Christian standards.

It is hard to imagine a more powerful form of moral influence on teenagers than the following. Visualize an adult-youth discussion on personal morals, where honesty becomes the topic. A well-known and a well-respected man or woman rises and reports that he or she was subtly requested to be dishonest in the workplace. The speaker refused and then explains why and what happened as a result of that stand.

2. Become Co-Producers of Morals for Society

Personal moral issues will always be high on young people's agendas. This is because they are feeling their freedom and are slowly taking responsibility for their own opinions. They are being pressed on every side to respond in some way to drinking alcohol, using drugs, and so on, but it would be a serious mistake to limit our concern for moral growth to the personal realm. Morals relate to what a society stands for, as the Bible affirms over and over again. In the Old Testament, Israel is to be an example to all the nations. In the New Testament, the church is to be the body of Christ ministering to the world.

The challenge to adults is how to connect our beliefs about God with moral issues we have in common with all people. This is difficult to do in our secular society. Many adults formulate their morals for society on the basis of what is good for business or what they hear in the community. If these secular-oriented adults are church members, they either separate their beliefs about God from their social ethics or they attempt to interpret theology to support their opinions about society. In either case they fail to understand that Christian morals must start with our beliefs about God.

Adults in congregations are expected to translate Christian beliefs into morals for contemporary situations, but they seldom do so in a deliberate, systematic manner. Rather, they talk about social ethics informally without trying to arrive at a position, or they take a position on issues such as abortion or public housing for low-income people if that issue is pressed on them from secular sources. If the congregation is going to be a moral community as described in chapter 2, and a place where such morals are practiced as suggested in chapter 3, a rather large percentage of adults in a congregation must devote a considerable amount of time working on what theological beliefs mean for moral practices in our secular world.

Adults can and should turn theology into morals for themselves in their regular classes, but adults could be of even greater service to the congregation if they saw this work as an opportunity to influence teenagers. How to proceed would depend on the size and resources of the congregation. In a small or medium-size congregation the group might consist of an adult class and all the teenagers. In a large congregation a special group of adults and teenagers could be assembled. The purpose would be to hold a discussion of certain theological beliefs and the morals that follow from them, in order to learn how to think about moral situations.

This classroom process whereby teenagers interact with adults in the congregation on topics about which both are concerned is a way of taking teenagers seriously and of allowing adults to share the meaning of their faith. Moreover, the process helps teenagers use and test their developing mental abilities in a community that cares, both about them and about the welfare of society.

If circumstances permit, a more effective use of reason and discussion would be to start the whole enterprise as one in which adults and young people are going to be "co-producers" of morals. If everyone involved looked on this project as an opportunity to formulate provisional standards for the congregation, there would be an openness to one another and a sense of ownership of the final product. We should not expect such a group to write a comprehensive social ethic; that goal would be too ambitious. Since the purpose is to learn how to relate theological beliefs to contemporary moral situations, the group could take one theological principle and work on its meaning for today. In order to keep the discussion focused and provide a sense of progress, the group could start out with the goal of producing a statement of a theological principle and what that principle means for Christian social policies in their congregation. When complete, the statement would not be binding on anyone; it would be a carefully considered opinion that most people in the group believed to be appropriate.

The five general principles that follow are based on Christian beliefs. After a brief discussion of each principle, some implications for moral issues are suggested. If an adult-youth class adopts the project of co-producing a moral standard for a congregation, it is important to work from beliefs to morals. Such a class might select one of these five as an area to practice producing morals for a congregation.

Creation is good. The natural world, however, contains many elements that are cruel and undesirable, such as earthquakes, volcanoes, and hurricanes and other sudden shifts in weather. Animals have no concern for one another because nature endowed each species with instincts to prey on others. Although we do not understand why nature is so hostile or where nature will go in the future, we affirm that what God created is good and should be used in a careful way. This leads to concern for the physical environment and to a desire to protect and preserve the resources of our life.

God is concerned about all people. The characteristics of many different races in the world can be understood through the way each race has adapted to its environment. But the religions of different races and nations are more difficult to comprehend. Christians believe that somehow in the providence of God these differences have a purpose. Our responsibility in the light of the differences and of conflicts among people is to work for peace so that these matters can be resolved in a way that honors God's concern for all people. But peace will not come, nor will it be maintained, unless there is justice, and achieving justice is extremely complicated.

The basis on which just decisions are made is not easily agreed on. Should justice be based on equality (everyone treated the same), need (people treated according to their life situations such as age, sex, educational background, and financial status), or merit (those who try harder or work harder deserve more)? In a family or congregational situation, the basis of justice is subordinated to love. If a child has special needs due to illness or accident or if a family in a congregation has come on hard times, the loving basis of justice is need. But in other family and congregational situations, love would motivate treatment based on equality or merit. The selection of the basis of justice when we know the people in a personal way can be done with common sense and experience.

The problem of justice is much more complex when we are dealing with people in impersonal ways, through laws, or are trying to find a just solution to conflict between groups of people. Many times the issue is economic or political power, and those in power do not easily give it up or use it for the benefit of all people. In such cases, about all that justice can accomplish is some harmony in society or between warring groups.

Christians—through their individual positions in society and together in their congregations—should work for social justice because God is lord of all people. What should be done in any given impersonal situation where we are trying to bring about some harmony is open to considerable controversy. This is due in part to differences of opinion as to the basis on which we should act and also because we do not know exactly what the response will be in large impersonal situations. But these uncertainties should not lead to inaction or despair. What is unjust is usually fairly clear, and what can be done to relieve at least a part of the injustice is also fairly obvious. Missionaries, for example, have for a long time helped to develop agriculture, start schools, and found hospitals to serve the basic human needs of a people regardless of the oppressive nature of their society. In recent times Christians have supported efforts to supply food for famine victims and economic aid to help poor countries, even though their economic or political system was not to our liking. Many congregations have been concerned with the hungry and homeless people in their community and have responded as best they could to alleviate these harsh conditions. These efforts may not get to the root of the problem, but Christians feel that something can be done at the point of need because God is concerned about the condition of all people.

Government is to serve as well as protect people. A great part of government is devoted to keeping order inside the nation and protecting the nation from foreign powers. But after those efforts have been made, the government still has enormous influence on our lives. Because we live in a democracy, we elect our leaders, all the way from those who set public school policies in our communities to the President of the United States. This means that congregations have an opportunity to sensitize their members to many issues arising out of their concern for the welfare of all people, such as race relations, civil rights, tax policies, educational opportunities for all children, and fair employment practices.

Happy, healthy family life is basic for good child development and human relations. The Christian ideal is a husband and wife sharing the responsibility for the rearing of children and training them in faith and morals. The actual situation in the United States at this time is that about one-half of all marriages end in divorce. This translates into a high percentage of our adult population having gone through a wrenching emotional experience. Children of divorced parents have their family life disrupted and then reformulated; if the guardian parent remarries, there are more adjustments.

In addition to divorce, modern family life is under constant pressure if both parents work outside the home. There is less supervision of children and a rushed home schedule, so that the amount and quality of time available for conversation, play, and the enjoyment of simple pleasures is limited. Children with unsupervised time are more exposed to and influenced by television and by their peers than by their parents.

We need not continue to inventory all the forces in our culture that work against good marriages and against the proper development of children and youth. Readers can supply many such conditions from their own experience. What is necessary is for Christians to remind themselves that they must do all they can to help children and youth receive the love, discipline, and guidance they need in order to become mature, responsible people. In practical terms this means that congregations could sponsor day-care centers where religion as well as supervision is supplied, support Christian counseling centers, and provide reading materials, video cassettes, and other resources for home use. Congregations that take seriously the home as the first place where morals are formed and strengthened will find particular ways they can assist families in this matter.

All individuals are children of God. The Christian religion is individualistic in the sense that it expects people at some point after they reach the age of accountability—usually in adolescence—to make a confession of their faith in Jesus Christ as their lord and savior and to join a congregation where they will be encouraged to live by Christian virtues.

Christians believe each person is valuable in the eyes of God. Every person, even up to the moment of death, can confess faith in Christ, as is illustrated by the story of the thief who died on a cross beside Jesus. This leads Christians to a concern for the spiritual welfare of all persons, motivated in part by an evangelistic goal. If non-Christians experience the love of God through relationships with Christians, they may desire to become Christians. This is motivated in part by the belief that each person was made in the image of God and that to help another person in need is to serve God (Matt. 25:31–46). This moral principle leads Christians into many kinds of good deeds done on a personal basis. It also leads individuals and congregations to support fair housing laws, supply tutors for children whose parents are unable to help them with schoolwork, provide food for the unemployed, set up clinics for children, and serve God in other ways by helping people in need.

3. Suggest Go-and-See Activities

To go and see something of ethical significance is to participate in the matter. This partial participation is not as effective educationally as the involvement described in chapter 6, but go-and-see activities make it possible to broaden teenagers' experience in areas in which they cannot fully participate.

Go-and-see activities are usually trips to places where something of ethical importance is taking place. The following illustrations suggest the range and type of activities that could lead to a careful discussion of the question, "What should we do about _____ because of our faith in God?"

1. Visit a city council or state legislature when a topic teenagers understand is being debated. Adults will need to brief the teenagers on procedures and help them follow the debate.

2. Visit a local court where a teenager is on trial. Juvenile courts are often closed to the public, but trials of persons sixteen years or older are usually public. The trial should have some point that would motivate church teenagers to study the issues involved. If the charge was selling drugs, the teenagers—in addition to noting all that goes on in the courtroom—might interview the police officers who specialize in drug abuse. From this exploration, the teenagers could bring back to the larger group a report on what is actually happening with drug abuse in their town.

3. Go-and-see projects include interviews. If a youth group was interested in medical ethics concerning abortion, the right to die, or euthanasia, their discussion would be enlivened if a team of two or three teenagers interviewed medical doctors, ministers, social workers, or others who are involved with people who make those decisions. To obtain the best results about moral issues of this kind, a team of teenagers should study the issue and work out a list of questions they want to ask. Adults working with the team would

need to know the people in the community who are capable of—and interested in—responding to teenagers and also would make arrangements for a good interview. Teenagers need adults who will help them with an interview but will not take over or dominate the exchange. If a team spent a few weeks on a medical issue and interviewed some people with experience in the matter, the team should share its findings and suggestions with other teenagers or even with an adult group in the church.

4. Help Analyze Moral Dilemmas

Do stories about a moral dilemma (such as "Is it right to steal food if you are starving?") have a place in moral education? Such moral dilemmas can be used easily in classrooms, where student answers can be the basis for general discussion. Or an adult leader of a church youth group can clip newspaper or magazine stories containing a moral dilemma and use them to start a discussion. Such discussions can be helpful if the leader constantly asks the teenagers, "Why do you resolve the dilemma that way?" By getting the basis for decision out in the open where everyone can recognize it, the leader can help the group analyze its merit in relation to Christian beliefs.

The best source for contemporary moral dilemmas is newspapers. Almost every day—certainly every week—a story will appear that presents a serious ethical issue about which someone made a decision. A story that makes news usually has considerable human appeal and is therefore easy to use as a way to open a discussion. For example, at the time this is being written the story of the pink daiquiri is being widely discussed.

This is what happened. A woman went to a bar in Seattle and ordered a pink daiquiri. The waiter, noting that she was pregnant, asked her if she was sure she wanted an alcoholic drink. She repeated her order. A second waiter took the label off a bottle of beer which warns that alcohol is dangerous for a fetus. He placed the label before her, saying, "Just in case you didn't know." The woman was so angry she complained to the manager of the bar, who promptly fired the two waiters.

Many moral points have been noted by newspaper writers. (1) Does Congress have a right to warn prospective mothers about the harm of drinking alcohol? (2) If the waiters had not warned the pregnant woman and the baby was born defective, could she sue the waiters for not warning her? (3) Does the woman have a right to treat her body as she pleases, and if so, what right does the unborn baby have? (4) One columnist was very upset about this incident. She wrote that the pregnant woman has a right to do wrong and should be free to drink alcohol or smoke even though she knows these things will harm her unborn child. Do you agree? (5) Does the manager of the bar have a right to fire the two waiters? They did not say they would not serve her, they only warned her of the danger. (6) If the woman comes back to the bar a month later and orders a drink for herself and a small amount of beverage alcohol to put in the baby's bottle "because it quiets him and puts him to sleep," should the waiters refuse? Or does a mother have a right to determine the food and drink of her child?

Another source of topics for group discussion is teenagers themselves. They are alert to many problems that perplex them and are knowledgeable about situations to which people have responded in a certain way. Several young people could probably develop a "case" in a rather short time. The adult leader should go over the material in advance to be sure it is suitable for instructional purposes.

Discussion of cases from the newspaper or from the young people's ideas can easily become an exchange of opinions without much thought. The leader must not only ask "Why do you hold that position?" but must also attempt to get the group to make a judgment about the preferred position from the standpoint of the Christian faith. It is sometimes helpful to stop a discussion and ask each person to write what he or she thinks is the right view for the congregation. A sharing of those thoughts may help the group focus on the welfare of the congregation rather than only on the rights of individuals.

CHAPTER 8

Toward
Christian Character

In the first chapter of this book we distinguished the conventional morals of society from Christian morals derived from our religious beliefs. Often the two overlap, for our conventional morals and many of our laws have been influenced by Christianity. Sometimes the two are in conflict, as illustrated by the civil rights movement of the 1960s. Black students in Greensboro, North Carolina, defied conventional morals and civil law when they sat down at a public lunchroom and requested service; the morals of the students came from their Christian beliefs and were nurtured and supported by congregations.

In succeeding chapters we discussed the congregation as the place where teenagers could come of age and grow morally if the congregation was a place where morals were deliberately formed and practiced.

In this final chapter we will note the importance of the congregation in the formation of Christian character.

What Is Character?

Character means a set of enduring personal traits. The students who started the sit-in method of social protest not only had moral standards, they also had courage and confidence in their nonviolent strategy. We must be careful not to assume that character traits are good or bad without considering the context in which they operate. Remember, a person can be trustworthy and still be a criminal. The folk saying "There is honor among thieves" reflects the need of criminals to trust one another in order to work as a team. Or there may be some circumstances when one may have to lie in order to save innocent people.

Formed in Early Childhood

Our character begins to take shape soon after we are born. We are formed, shaped, and influenced by parents, playmates, neighbors, schools, churches, children's clubs, television, and other social forces. We are hardly conscious of what we absorb from parents and others in our early years. Almost all the major decisions we make about how we use our time and money, how we relate to other people, the goals we set and the means we use to reach those goals, our work habits, the care we take of our environment, the way we use the natural resources of the earth, and the value we place on human life are directly related to character traits formed in early childhood.

During the first five or six years we learn patterns of thought and action to fit various situations. Behind these outward patterns are sentiments or emotionally charged styles of responding. Children by this age have identifiable character traits. One child may be kind, thoughtful, and cooperative. Another may be angry much of the time, yet honest and intelligent; another may be shy, diffident, and easily diverted from one thing to another. At this stage personality and character traits are diffuse, but an underlying assumption about how one is to get along with others is being formed. These underlying sentiments are sometimes referred to as the ''basic assumptions'' people bring to decision-making. These assumptions or sentiments are established in early childhood by rewards given for behavior that is approved, by punishment for behavior that is disapproved, and by the way parents and peers model conduct in specific life situations. Concern for others, for example, is learned in a home environment by the way a child is treated by parents and by the way parents coach the child to respond to the needs of others. Carolyn, age three, was playing with her grandfather in the living room when suddenly there was a scream from the bathroom where Ian, age six, had fallen. Carolyn stopped playing and said to her grandfather, ''Ian is hurt. I go see if I can help. I be back in a few minutes.'' She returned and said, ''Ian is OK,'' and resumed her play. By age three Carolyn had learned to care and instantly applied it to a concrete life situation. In this same manner other sentiments, such as kindness, sharing, thankfulness, respect for living things (pets), and curiosity begin in the first few years of life and characterize a child by the age of six. Less desirable sentiments, such as disregard for a brother or sister, cruelty to living things, or an inordinate desire to have all the toys are learned in the same way.

During middle childhood, ages six through ten, children expand the implications of their sentiments to different life situations. Robert Coles, professor of child psychiatry at Harvard University, who supervised the first survey of "the beliefs and moral values of America's children" reported that by the age of ten children have a moral compass by which they make moral decisions. Moreover, the basic assumptions and beliefs they have acquired by that age are more important to their moral character than are factors such as gender, income of family, race, or ethnic origin.[1] The five types of moral compass that children use by the age of ten are as follows:

1. Civic humanist (25%), in which moral judgments are made according to what is regarded as serving the common goods of the neighborhood, town, or the nation at large—they would "do what would be best for everyone involved."
2. Conventionalist (20%), in which moral judgments are made in accord with what is generally accepted in the community as a given—the accepted social practices—especially as they are mediated through such authority figures as parents and teachers—they would "follow the advice of an authority such as a parent, teacher or youth leader."
3. Expressivist (18%), in which moral judgments are made in accord with the satisfaction of certain emotional feelings and psychological needs—they would "do what makes [them] happy."
4. Theistic (16%), in which moral judgments are made in accordance with a religious authority, such as scripture, authoritative teaching, or the traditions of the religious community—they would "do what God or scripture tells [them] is right."
5. Utilitarian (10%), in which moral judgments are made in accord with the practical advantages they afford the individual—that is, on the basis of how a particular decision would serve the person's self-interests—they would "do what would improve [their] situation or get [them] ahead."[2]

The types of moral orientation and the percentage of children in each type should not surprise us. The children reflect what we see in

America today, where values are becoming more secular. If we combine the civic humanist, conventional, and theistic types, almost
two thirds of the children considered the welfare of others in their
moral decisions, so there is considerable altruistic residue from our
religious past. Moreover, the language of religion and church attendance continues. Eighty-two percent of the children said they believed in God, 57 percent said they attended a religious service at
least once a week, 39 percent indicated they prayed daily, and 34
percent claimed a life-changing religious experience. These percent-
ages indicate a very religious group; yet only 2 percent would look to
God for advice, and only 3 percent would go to a religious leader for
help on a moral issue. The huge gap between the high percentage of
children who voiced a religious interest and their use of religion to
help them with moral dilemmas led the researchers to wonder
whether religion for this group is not a "wallpaper factor": something that is in the background but is not important for decision-
making.[3]

The Gallup organization, which has been questioning adults
about their religion for over five decades, has come to the same con-
clusion. They report that 92 percent of Americans state a religious
preference, 68 percent say they are members of a church or syna-
gogue, and 56 percent say religion is very important in their lives.
But they summarize America's religious life in this way: "While religion is highly popular in America, it is to a large extent superficial; it
does not change people's lives to the degree one would expect from
their level of professed faith."[4]

The findings of the Harris survey and the Gallup polls show that
America's history of religious influence in our culture continues in
the public consciousness. Teenagers pick up and affirm this "people's religion" from adults, schools, political speeches, and observations of the work of churches and religious organizations. This form
of religion is more of a reverence for American values than it is faith
in God, but it does influence the morals of older children and teenagers. The Harris survey researchers found, for example, that no
matter which moral compass the children used, if they attended
church frequently, "the less likely they will be willing to cheat, lie or
steal, drink alcohol underage, or be libertarian in their decisions
about their sexual behavior. This suggests that religious institutions
have a moral influence even for those whose moral assumptions are
not religiously oriented."[5]

This connection between strong religious beliefs and moral decisions is to be expected, for religion shapes the believer's life. But the Harris survey does not provide data on what religion means in terms of attitudes toward people of other religions, races, or ethnic origins. Some people, motivated by their beliefs, are prejudiced against certain other people or may have acquired a legalistic code of morals without regard for mercy or forgiveness. In his comprehensive study of prejudice, Gordon Allport found there were two kinds of religiosity. One was negative in that members were trained to despise or belittle people of other religious, racial, or ethnic groups. The other was positive in that members were helped to overcome selfish impulses and were trained to think about their moral principles within the context of what was good for society.[6] There have been times in the past when Christian churches have supported racial prejudice or denied equality to women, and these attitudes still come to the fore in contemporary church life. Having strong religious beliefs, therefore, does not guarantee that the resulting moral standards will be Christian. Religious beliefs and the morals they produce must be under constant review in order for them to be what God wants for the present.

Tested in Adolescence
The term "moral compass" used in the Harris survey is a good description of what children use in moral decision-making when they enter the teen years. A compass needle points to the north because of invisible magnetic force. A moral compass influences the choices a person makes by silently but constantly urging him or her to act on the basis of an assumption or sentiment that has been accepted as "right." This does not mean, however, that people with the same moral compass will agree on what should be done in specific cases. Take the civic-humanist orientation, for example. Two people with this basic assumption might disagree on what kind of program for the homeless was "best for everyone involved." The same is true for those who have a theistic orientation. Two people with equal devotion to God may disagree on "what God or scripture tells [them] is right."

Therefore, we have two major areas of life related to morals that are tested during the teen years. One area is the basic assumptions or set of character traits a person uses to make moral decisions. This area is difficult and slow to change because it is subjective, being rooted in one's early childhood. We are often not conscious of our character traits, except that we do not "feel" right if we don't live according to these traits. The second area of testing is the way a person uses reason, imagination, and judgment to apply that basic assumption to a situation about which a decision must be made. This area is easier to change because it is objective; it is based on reason. Moreover, we are conscious of the way we analyze a situation, select facts, and reason about the outcome. These mental processes are open, so our peers can challenge or agree with the way we make decisions.

Adults who want to influence the character development of teenagers are tempted to work through reason. This comes about, as discussed in chapters 5 and 7, because teenagers are discovering their ability to reason abstractly, to understand history, and to think of conditions of life different from what they see about them. So they use their knowledge of different life-styles they see on TV or in high school groups to argue about the morals they acquired in childhood. Adults, realizing that teenagers are growing up and being accustomed to reasoning with other adults about morals, often assume that reasoning about morals is the way to influence character development. Moreover, data gathering, observation of conditions, and reasoning about these things are so important for adult decisions that we tend to think the application of reason to moral issues will bring us to a position on which most people will agree. Such is not the case, and we need to understand why this is so.

The Limits of Reason

Let's first consider why reason most often defers to the affections and then note the inability of reason to select the basis on which to make moral judgments.

Reason Defers to the Affections

Reason is relatively weak in comparison to the affections. As already indicated, by the time individuals are conscious of their ability to reason about their moral choices, they are involved in a struggle between what they want and what other people expect. Reason is most often used to justify or explain actions they have taken or plan to take rather than to provide guidance for actions they ought to take.

The affections, in addition to being formed first and being opera-
tive long before objective reasoning is available, are more dynamic
than reason because of the way they were formed within us. We
have already discussed many specific matters, such as how we use
our time and money and how we relate to other people. In general
terms we are talking about sentiments: what people like or dislike,
what they give themselves to or avoid. The emotions associated
with ideas, relationships, and possessions are deeply ingrained.
During adolescence and adulthood one can use reason to modify
these emotionally charged attitudes, but it takes time and much conscious effort for reason to make much change. The following illustrations may help.

If children are raised to believe that people of a certain color are
inferior to themselves, or if they are trained to be suspicious of people with a certain religion, they will have great difficulty reasoning
their way out of these prejudices when they become adults.

If, in their early childhood, persons were vigorously and system-
atically taught that they must obey people in authority—such as
teachers, police, judges, elected officials, and job bosses— such people will tend to obey those authorities even though their reason tells
them the orders are immoral, offensive, or illegal. The power of this
obedient sentiment over reason was demonstrated by an experiment conducted by Stanley Milgram, a professor at Yale University.
Milgram recruited men, ordinary citizens ages twenty to fifty,
through a newspaper advertisement offering to pay a small fee if
they would participate in a "memory" experiment. When these citizens arrived, they were introduced to a man who was to be the
learner. It was explained that this was an experiment in the effects of
punishment for not learning. The learner was to memorize a certain
response to a word, and if he made a mistake, the citizen was to pun-
ish him with an electric shock. The learner was strapped in a chair
with wires attached to a lever in an adjoining room where the citizen
could administer shocks from 15 to 450 volts, labeled from slight to
extreme shock.

The learner was actually an actor employed for this role. There
was no electricity in the wires, hence no danger, but the citizen who
was recruited through the newspaper ad thought he was actually
causing the punishment.

When during the experiment the learner made mistakes, the director told the citizen to increase the electrical shock. Citizens, when

left alone, would usually use only mild voltage, but when the director was present and told them to increase the shock, about 65 percent obeyed up to the level of extreme shock, even though some of them showed tension by sweating, groaning, or biting their lips as they obeyed the director. In order to test further the way ordinary citizens obey people in authority, the experiment was done in a different place to eliminate the prestige of Yale University, but the results were about the same.

In order to test what would happen if the citizens were physically close to the learner and saw the effects of the electrical punishment, the citizens were moved closer in various stages. When the citizens got nearer to the victim, the number who would administer severe shock decreased. But even when the citizens were holding the hand of the victim while they administered the shock, one third would obey orders to increase the voltage. If the director left the room or gave orders by phone, they would be less likely to administer severe shock.[7]

The original Milgram experiment, and later variations, show that ordinary citizens do not like to cause suffering, yet a high percentage will do so when following orders from a higher authority. This explains the behavior of some well-educated, responsible people who have done the same thing in a real situation. At the Nuremberg trials, Nazi generals and high officials argued they were not to be blamed for killing millions of Jews because they were just obeying orders. Major executives in American corporations, when caught illegally fixing prices or cheating on government military contracts, have also responded that they were just following orders. Top governmental officials involved in the Iran-Contra affair during the Reagan presidency argued in court that they should not be held accountable for their action because they were just obeying their superiors. These cases involve well-educated, intelligent men holding high office, yet they were more influenced by their training to obey than they were by their reason.

A more common example of how one's sentiment takes precedent over reason is that of men and women who find themselves in an almost impossible marriage situation. The woman may be abused or the man constantly depreciated, yet they stay in the miserable marriage. Why is their reason unable to free them? In many cases it is because the man or the woman has been brought up to believe that marriage is sacred and the vows taken before God and

friends are not to be broken. These beliefs and the emotional ener-
gies supporting them can keep the couple in a relationship that reason has judged they should abandon.

Reason Cannot Make Commitments

The second limit of reason in ethical matters is its inability in many
cases to select a basis for making judgments. Everyone will agree
that peace is better than war, food better than starvation, life better
than death, truth better than lies. The limits of reason emerge in specific cases in which we have to make a decision.

In the case of war, the issue is the purpose of the war. Most people in the United States considered World War II a tragic necessity in
order to stop the expansion of Nazi Germany. But some people refused to fight in that war, not because the cause was wrong but because they considered killing to be wrong. If people have been
brought up to consider killing other people wrong and have a strong
feeling about this conviction, are they not as reasonable about their
refusal to kill in war as those who are willing to kill in order to stop
Nazism?

In the case of food, the issue is that some people have an ample
supply while others are in need. Ordinary sympathy would suggest
a sharing of food with those in need. But note that one has to use a
sentiment word—sympathy—rather than a reasoned argument to
motivate sharing. Reason by itself would advise those with food to
keep it, for their supply might run out.

In the case of abortion the issue is: Whose rights are to be protected? The pro-life position is reasonable, once one has assumed
that human life starts with conception and that such life has a right
to continue. The pro-choice position is equally logical, once one has
assumed that the mother has a right to choose whether or not she
wants a child. Reason can justify either position, once one has decided the basis for selecting a position on the issue. The basis on
which a person decides is not reason but conscience, religion, relationship with other people, concerns for society, devotion to the
idea of individual rights, or other beliefs and sentiments that make
up the deeper levels of one's self.

Even telling the truth cannot always be decided by reason. We
know that truth-telling is extremely important. We cannot maintain
personal relations without mutual trust, which comes from practicing honesty. We cannot maintain a social order if we cannot expect

and require truthfulness. Most of the time we communicate truthfully with others. But there are times when telling the truth becomes an issue about which we have to make a decision.

Such a situation occurred in World War II when Nazi soldiers in France and Holland asked householders if Jews were living with them. Some householders who were harboring Jews lied to the Nazis in order to protect the Jews. Almost everyone looking back on that situation approves of lying under those conditions. But some householders did not lie, and the Jews in those houses were taken away. In both cases the issue was not decided by reason. Reason was auxiliary to the character traits of the householder. Both groups thought about the situation in which they found themselves. Those who lied to protect their Jewish guests did so for some belief such as "these Jews are innocent and deserve the right to live." That belief was also linked with some character trait such as courage, for these people risked their own lives with the idea that Nazism was an evil that must be resisted. Those who told the truth and revealed the presence of Jews did so for some belief such as "the Nazi state had the right to rule" and probably out of fear for their own situation if they did not obey. We do not know exactly what the deep inner emotions were in the lives of those who resisted or acquiesced to the Nazi demand, but reason did not select the option they chose. Reason only helped to analyze the situation and justify the options. The real source of the decision came from the deeper levels of their being.

Context for Character Development

This discussion on the limits of reason in moral matters is not intended to show the superiority of one's assumptions or affections over reason. The purpose is to caution us about the role of reason, since that ability develops so rapidly during the teen years and is so valued and needed in our complex society. We should constantly remind ourselves that moral decisions and actions involve the whole person. In fact, moral decisions always involve a struggle. One part of the self wants gratification and comfort, another part reminds us to be caring for others, while our mind tries to decide what is right given the conditions we face.

The struggle to be a moral person and to apply morals properly to practical problems is common to teenagers and adults. Both need the stabilizing influence and guidance that comes from participating in the worship and work of a congregation. Adults who want to influence the character development of young people should use their time and energy to help the congregation be a Christian community.

This emphasis on the central place of the congregation does not mean that the morals of individuals are to be set by the congregation. Rather, it means the congregation is the place for individuals to work out their moral standards with other believers who struggle with the same issues and common concerns.

It is the Christians' belief in God that sets their moral standards apart from the morals of secular society. Christian morals are motivated by, and deeply influenced by, a believer's relation to God. One's morality does not start with a list of do's and don'ts but with an effort to discern the will of God for the situation in which one must act. This is why the history of Christianity records remarkable stories of people who sacrificed their personal comfort or put their lives at risk for various causes in order to please God. Moreover, a countless number of Christian people quietly live altruistic, self-giving lives today because that is their response to the love, guidance, and comfort they have received from God. So Christian morals are the result of a relationship with God and arise out of one's spiritual life. Christians are responsible *to* God for the way they live. This orientation of oneself toward God, and a belief that judgment comes from God according to the way one orders one's life, is the center from which Christian moral conduct flows. Christians, however, do not face life alone. Their lives have always been shared in the congregations where they worship and work out the meaning of their faith for contemporary situations. The characteristics of the congregation as a community are of critical importance in nurturing the moral life of its members and for providing a setting in which together they can think about their responsibility to God.

Paul, who had to deal with this matter in the congregations he founded, identified love as the major characteristic of congregational life. Without love, our speech, wisdom, knowledge, faith, and even self-sacrifice will be of little value in a congregation (1 Cor. 13:1–3). This fundamental attitude of concern for one another was a response to God's love for humankind shown in God's having sent Jesus to save us from sin and to show us the style of life God desires (Rom. 5:1–11). The congregation was a special society where love was the "more excellent way" to live (1 Cor. 12:31–14:1). Paul's master virtue for the church is in harmony with Jesus' Great Commandments recorded in the Gospels: "You shall love the Lord your God with all your heart, and with all your soul, and with all your mind, and with all your strength. . . . You shall love your neighbor as yourself" (Mark 12:30–31).

Victor Furnish has identified sixteen virtues in the letters of Paul. The virtues are grouped around three themes: (1) love expressed in terms such as long-suffering, kindness, peace, gentleness, goodness, and self-control (2 Cor. 6:6; Gal. 5:22); (2) purity (2 Cor. 6:6; Phil. 4:8); and (3) truthfulness expressed in knowledge and faithfulness (2 Cor. 6:6; Phil. 4:8).

It is important to note, as Furnish points out, that Paul's list of virtues is not a list of moral duties or ideals toward which individuals should strive in order to have a good character. Rather, the lists, such as the one in Galatians 5:22–23, are "the fruit of the Spirit." The Holy Spirit is God's presence and power in the church; as its believers participate in the worship and work of the church, they increasingly practice the virtues that help the community be what God desires.[8]

Vices are the opposite of virtues. Vices create fear and distrust and thus weaken, disrupt, or destroy community. Furnish points out that Paul's list of vices is mainly "social"—of the kinds of relationships that hurt congregations. Moreover, the lists of vices are tailored for the problems in the congregation to which he is writing. For example, in his second letter to the Corinthians, Paul lists quarreling, jealousy, anger, selfishness, slander, gossip, conceit, disorder, impurity, immorality, and licentiousness (2 Cor. 12:20–21). The list of vices he records in the church at Rome (Rom. 1:28–31) and at Galatia (Gal. 5:19–21) is written about people who do not "acknowledge" God, or if they know God, they pay no attention to God's will for human life.[9]

In the final analysis, Christians are responsible to God for their character and actions and are accountable to one another to build and maintain a community where Christian virtues are practiced and vices suppressed. A congregation with these characteristics will be the finest context in which teenagers and all other members can grow morally.

Leader's Guide

Audience

This book was written for adults who have a special interest in teen-agers and a concern for their moral development. Adult leaders of youth groups, teachers of youth classes, ministers, and parents of teenagers in their role as moral mentors may find help in this book. However, moral development as interpreted in this book assumes that certain societies—in the form of a close-knit group of people, a family, a church, a peer group, or some combination of these societies—transmit and have the possibility of transforming the moral standards by which we live. From the standpoint of the Christian religion, therefore, we must focus attention on the congregation, for that society is formed by believers and in turn influences their moral decisions. This book is designed for adult study groups, to help them understand their essential role in helping a congregation be a community that will guide teenagers' moral development.

The Classroom Situation

It is assumed that most adult classes have about forty minutes that can be devoted to study. More time is desirable, so try to schedule up to one hour for each session.

It is assumed that most adult classes will range in size from ten to twenty persons. For this size of class a general discussion method will work rather well. The leader should not allow any one or two persons to speak too often or too long. The leader can encourage others to respond, or the leader may ask some of the less-talkative adults to come to class with certain matters prepared in advance. Such assignments are suggested for each chapter in this guide.

If the class is larger than twenty-five to thirty people, the leader will probably need to use some small-group discussion methods in order to assure full participation. When a major point has been made, a basic question asked, or a provocative case presented, the class could be quickly formed into groups of four to six people for discussion. General discussion should then follow, based on what the smaller groups report to the whole class.

Use of This Book

A copy of this book should be ordered for every person in the class. Each chapter is short and is limited to a few major ideas. Leaders should not use class time going over what is in the book except to introduce the topic or to present their response to the text.

The reasons for supplying a book for each person are as follows: (1) Christian ethics is a complex subject and needs careful, reflective consideration. This type of study will not occur unless each person has taken time to focus attention on the material in the book. (2) If each person will read the assigned chapter in advance, all class time can be used to explore the topic. It is through the sympathetic understanding of the views of class members and a subordination of ourselves to what Christ wants for the world that we find "the mind of Christ" for our situation. (3) Each chapter is condensed and has few illustrations. If class members will note examples or illustrations in the margin or will underline parts with which they agree or disagree, they can quickly turn to that place to share their response during the class discussions.

Before the First Session

Plan the number of sessions you think desirable. This book assumes nine sessions: an introductory one to organize the class and explain the course and one for each of the eight chapters. A leader could expand several of the chapters into two parts for a total of ten or more periods. Chapters 2 and 3 contain a discussion of central issues in Christian ethics, and each could be easily expanded into two sessions. A good arrangement would be to plan for nine sessions but allow for several extra sessions if the class wants to expand the discussions of some chapters.

It is important for the leader to read the book in advance. Make a few notes on the content of each chapter so you will be able to point out what it is about and how each chapter fits into the overall course. Notice that most chapters start with a few sentences about the content of the chapter. Have your "overview" ready for the first session.

First Session
Introduction

Distribute the books. Allow time for everyone to read the Preface. Now turn through the book chapter by chapter. Make a few comments about the content of each chapter and how it fits into the whole treatment. This overview is very important. It will help class members get a general idea of what they will be reading and will prepare them for the class discussions.

Explain why everyone should read the assigned chapter in advance of the class session. Point out that you will not use class time to tell them what is in the textbook. Indicate that you plan to make some assignments each week, so that one or two members can think about some part of the chapter in advance in order to start discussion. This method of having a few members prepared to respond to something in the chapter will help keep the discussion close to the concerns of the class.

A good way to make the assignments is to write on a slip of paper what you want a member to do for the next class. You can give the slip to that member at the end of class without using class time. However, during this first class you will have time to explain the process. Read the assignments you want to make for the next session, which will be on chapter 1. Either ask for volunteers or pick out persons you think will take the assignment seriously and come to class with a response that will stimulate discussion.

Second Session
Chapter 1: Our Moral Nature

This chapter opens by defining two kinds of morals. (1) Conventional morals are those standards almost everyone follows without thinking. They are the accepted rules and patterns of behavior. (2) Morals (ethics) means we have thought about what we are doing and can offer reasons why we believe a certain way to act is right. Ask members to comment on the two kinds of morals until everyone has the distinctions clearly in mind.

Morals (ethics) become more complicated when we realize that many different groups of people can think about morals. Other religious groups develop moral standards, and even atheistic groups have developed their own ideas about what is right. In order to avoid these complications, we will stick to our special interest in Christian morals.

Two of the sections of this chapter merit special attention. You could assign someone to come prepared to start the discussion for each section, or you could lead the class by using the discussion questions suggested in the following paragraphs.

1. In the section "Society Can Influence the Church," there are illustrations of how medical science has changed the definition of death, how a writer aroused public consciousness about ecology, and how the feminist movement raised the awareness of women's rights. Each has had an impact on church morals. Do you think it was "right" for the church to change to meet these new conditions? Give several reasons for your answer. Are there some developments in modern society (such as permissiveness in sexual relations or our lavish use of natural resources) that the church should resist? Why?

2. In the sections "The Church Can Influence Society" and "Our Solution," the congregation is considered a powerful force for influencing adults and teenagers to act on their Christian beliefs. What kind of changes in society should Christians try to make today? Should a congregation take a position on a moral issue? If so, name one or two moral issues of this type. The chapter concludes with the affirmation that congregations can make a powerful impression on teenagers if they translate their beliefs into moral practices. Why do congregations have so much trouble identifying a moral issue and then formulating a Christian response?

Third Session
Chapter 2: A Moral Community

The purpose of this chapter is to show that the congregation ought consciously to understand itself as a community where ethical judgments are processed and a moral style of life is high on everyone's agenda. The major part of class time should be spent on "Congregational Responsibility." Since this section should apply to your congregation, it may be desirable to divide the class into groups of four to six people. Ask the groups to rate the congregation on a scale of 1 (low) to 10 (perfect) on how close it is to being a Christian community and what can be done to improve the rating. After about ten minutes have the groups report to the whole class.

Keep the class in the small-group arrangement and ask them to consider this question: Is it possible to explore the "will of God" for this congregation? If so, what would have to be done to make that question the decisive matter in issues facing the congregation and the community in which it is located? After ten minutes have a general discussion based on the group reports.

If you do not want to use this method, you could conduct a general discussion based on reports individuals bring to the following assignments.

1. Jesus said that the basis of Christian decision-making should be "the will of God." This sounds rather clear-cut, but the section "A Concern for Moral Decision-Making" says congregational decision-making is often tentative and may be something of a compromise. Why was there such a gap between Jesus' teaching and the church in New Testament times? Does this gap exist today? What can be done about it?

2. The section "Individual Responsibility" assumes an individual who is highly motivated to please God. Is this an unrealistic assumption for church members? If so, how can we expect the congregation to be a community concerned about Christian morals? Would it help to form a small group of adults who would commit themselves to a prayerful consideration of moral issues?

Fourth Session
Chapter 3: A Practice of Moral Living

This chapter discusses two of the most difficult problems in faith and morals. The first is the tension between Christianity as it is institutionalized in the church and faith in God. The second is the tension between the morals the church teaches and what it actually does in its life and work. These problems are found throughout the Bible, and they will continue for a long time. What we can do at the present about these problems is to refresh our minds about the way sin and human mistakes constantly hamper our efforts to be the kind of community we ought to be. For this purpose you might assign one person to review and comment on the "Institutional Religion" section, followed by discussion, and another person to review the "Practicing Morals" section.

The last section of the chapter, "Learning by Involvement," is designed to show how teenagers are becoming alert to all that goes on in the congregation. The leader may want to summarize this situation and remind the class of the church's opportunity to be a caring community for teenagers as the teenagers move into adulthood.

Fifth Session
Chapter 4: Coming of Age—Social Setting

The purpose of this chapter and the next is to interpret the teen years as a major opportunity to influence the moral life of individuals. Since everyone in the class has been through this period of life, you may want to use a guided discussion method. If so, divide the available time into two parts. Use the first part to discuss the developments in American society since 1900 that have created our technical and scientific society. Since this kind of society requires workers with a lot of education and training, the preparation time has been getting longer. Moreover, the separation between those who will manage this kind of society and those who cannot do more than simple work is becoming greater.

Assign someone to study the section "Society Defines Adolescence." Ask that person to come prepared to report on the way high school students understand the long period of preparation for their vocation.

Use the second time period to focus attention on the social situation of teenagers in your congregation. Discuss briefly the data from Francis Ianni's research showing that most of the assumptions teenagers have about how to live come from the group with which they identify themselves.

Assign someone to review the five characteristics of teenagers in our middle-class churches and come prepared to give reasons for agreeing or disagreeing with each one. Follow this presentation with a general discussion.

Sixth Session
Chapter 5: Coming of Age—Self-Discovery

So much has been written about the personal aspects of teenagers' development that everyone in the class may want to talk. Perhaps you should allocate about half the available time for a general discussion of teenagers' struggle to answer the "Who am I?" question.

Class members should be able to respond from their own experience without making assignments in advance.

The next section under "Help" discusses four groups that influence teenagers in their struggle to find the self they want to be. The congregation has a privileged position, for it can influence teenagers and their families; it can also sponsor a youth group. Assign someone to make an assessment of how well your congregation is using its privileged position. After this assessment has been shared with the class, ask others to give their opinion of how well your congregation influences its youth.

Seventh Session
Chapter 6: Helping Teenagers—Involvement

The purpose of this chapter is to put in priority order the ways adults can influence teenagers. The basic principle is the involvement of adults with teenagers in a variety of relationships. Involvement will, of course, include discussion of what is going on, but it is the adult sharing his or her faith and morals that makes involvement the preferred method of moral education. Because this principle is fundamental to this approach to helping teenagers grow morally, it should be discussed by the whole class. The leader could conduct this discussion or could assign a person to open the discussion with an answer to this question: Why is involvement with teenagers in significant church work the most effective way to teach Christian morals?

Talking about the four ways adults can be involved moves the discussion into the congregation's program. Since each congregation is different, the leader needs to decide what is most appropriate for the class. Many adults, especially in large congregations, may not know what is presently being done with teenagers. Someone who has this information should be asked to report. This person may be asked to suggest what more could be done to involve adults in the life of the young people. Follow this report with general discussion.

Eighth Session
Chapter 7: Helping Teenagers—Discussion

The four methods of discussing morals in this chapter apply equally to adults, so you may want to use the class period as an example of how important discussion can be for helping Christians become alert to moral issues. If you decide to use class time this way, you should select the topics carefully because many people in the class will want to express their opinions. For that reason you may want to schedule two sessions for this chapter. However, the following suggestions are for one session.

Assign someone to select one of the five theological principles in the chapter as a demonstration of how Christians should work from their beliefs to morals. This person should explain the principle and, perhaps, cite some biblical passages to illuminate it. Then the reporter should indicate what moral issues follow from the theological belief. After this report, lead a general discussion. Focus first on the theological statement. Why is it important? Do Christians take it seriously? Turn next to the moral issues. Are the issues from the reporter a proper deduction from the theological statement? Do more moral issues arise from this belief? If so, what are they? You might draw this section of the class to an end by briefly considering this question: To what extent does our congregation embody this theological principle and the moral standard that comes from it?

If there is time for further demonstration of how discussion can clarify and enrich our understanding of morals, use the case of the pink daiquiri. You can review the case quickly because the class members have already read it. Have the class turn to the six questions about this case and discuss them one by one.

You may need to remind the class that this session was an example of how important it is to discuss moral issues in a Christian context. This means individuals have an obligation to listen to the reasons of others as well as to state their own convictions.

Ninth Session
Chapter 8: Toward Christian Character

This final chapter brings the major themes of this book together with some new data and ideas.

The new data are in the section "Formed in Early Childhood." Have the class turn to those pages and review the list of five orientations. Remember, this is an analysis of all teenagers in America, not just the ones who attend church. However, a certain amount of this secular orientation is in our church youth.

These data lead us to realize that morals at their deepest level are formed by the people we associate with. Out of these associations we develop what we live for and what we resist. That is why the section on "The Limits of Reason" is of critical importance. Reason cannot easily change what we like and want or what we dislike or resist. Since this is the last meeting, you may want to lead a general discussion of this section. If not, assign someone to come prepared to respond to this section in order to start the thinking.

As leader you may want to conclude the class by putting the last section, "Context for Character Development," in your own words. This section affirms that the congregation is the group embodying Christian virtues and therefore is the place where teenagers at their deepest level of being are motivated to develop a Christian style of life.

Notes

CHAPTER 1
OUR MORAL NATURE

1. R. H. Tawney, *Religion and the Rise of Capitalism* (New York: Penguin Books, 1947), pp. 91–95.
2. Howard Zinn, *SNCC: The New Abolitionists* (Boston: Beacon Press, 1964), pp. 16–17.
3. *The Encyclopedia Americana,* 1986, vol. 6, p. 778.
4. Zinn, p. 19.

CHAPTER 2
A MORAL COMMUNITY

1. Paul L. Lehmann, *Ethics in a Christian Context* (New York: Harper & Row, 1963), pp. 131, 159.

CHAPTER 3
A PRACTICE OF MORAL LIVING

1. C. Ellis Nelson, *How Faith Matures* (Louisville, Ky.: Westminster/John Knox Press, 1989), pp. 42–59.
2. Carl S. Dudley, "Using Church Images for Commitment, Conflict, and Renewal," in *Congregations: Their Power to Form and Transform,* ed. C. Ellis Nelson (Atlanta, Ga.: John Knox Press, 1988), pp. 89–114.
3. Alasdair MacIntyre, *After Virtue,* 2nd ed. (Notre Dame, Ind.: University of Notre Dame Press, 1984), pp. 187–188.
4. Ibid., pp. 194–195.
5. C. Ellis Nelson, *How Faith Matures* (Louisville, Ky.: Westminster/John Knox Press, 1989), pp. 63–77.
6. Robert K. Merton, *Social Theory and Social Structure* (New York: Free Press, 1968), pp. 335–440.
7. Jerome Kagan, "A Conception of Early Adolescence," in *Daedalus,* Fall 1971, pp. 999–1001.

CHAPTER 4
COMING OF AGE—SOCIAL SETTING

1. Francis A. J. Ianni, *The Search for Structure* (New York: Free Press, 1989), pp. 22–54.

2. *The Works of Aristotle Translated Into English,* W. D. Ross, ed., vol. XI, *Rhetorica,* tr. W. Rhys Roberts (Oxford: Clarendon Press, 1946), 1389a–b. Reprinted by permission of Oxford University Press.

3. "Lessons in ethics might curb computer crime, experts say," *Austin American Statesman* 16 Mar. 1991, D2.

CHAPTER 5
COMING OF AGE—SELF-DISCOVERY

1. Erik H. Erikson, *Identity: Youth and Crisis* (New York: W. W. Norton & Co., 1968), pp. 128–179. For a critical review of the idea of "identity" as a social/psychological experience see Roy F. Baumeister, *Identity: Cultural Change and the Struggle for Self* (New York: Oxford University Press, 1986), pp. 198–232.

2. Erikson, pp. 174–176.

3. Statistics from *Girl Scouts Survey on the Beliefs and Moral Values of America's Children* (the Harris survey), Robert Coles, director (New York: Girl Scouts of the United States of America, 1989), pp. 11, 110. Reprinted by permission.

4. Douglas C. Kimmel and Irving B. Weiner, *Adolescence: A Developmental Transition* (Hillside, N.J.: Lawrence Erlbaum Associates, 1985), pp. 449–451.

5. Joseph Adelson, "The Development of Ideology in Adolescence," in *Adolescence in the Life Cycle: Psychological Change and the Social Context,* Sigmund E. Dragastin and Glen H. Elder, Jr., eds. (New York: John Wiley & Sons, 1975), pp. 63–78.

6. David R. Krathwohl, Benjamin S. Bloom, and Bertram B. Masia, *Taxonomy of Educational Objectives,* Handbook II: *Affective Domain* (New York: David McKay Co., 1969), pp. 176–193.

7. Adelson, pp. 70–71. See also John C. Coleman, *The Nature of Adolescence* (New York: Methuen, 1980), pp. 35–37.

8. Adelson, pp. 72–73.

CHAPTER 6
HELPING TEENAGERS—INVOLVEMENT

1. Raymond Montemayor, Gerald R. Adams, and Thomas P. Gullotta, eds., *From Childhood to Adolescence* (Newbury Park, Calif.: Sage Publications, 1990), p. 86.

2. John J. Conger and Anne C. Petersen, *Adolescence and Youth: Psychological Development in a Changing World,* 3rd ed. (San Francisco: Harper & Row, 1984), p. 208.

3. Search Institute, *Young Adolescents and Their Parents* (Minneapolis: Search Institute, 1984), p. 42.

4. Ibid., p. 46.

5. *Girl Scouts Survey on the Beliefs and Moral Values of America's Children* (New York: Girl Scouts of the United States of America, 1989), p. xv.

CHAPTER 7
HELPING TEENAGERS—DISCUSSION

1. ASCD Panel on Moral Education, *Moral Education in the Life of the School* (Alexandria, Va.: Association for Supervision and Curriculum Development, 1988), p. 27.

2. Search Institute, *Young Adolescents and Their Parents* (Minneapolis: Search Institute, 1984), p. 40.

3. The Harris survey is entitled *Girl Scouts Survey on the Beliefs and Moral Values of America's Children* (New York: Girl Scouts of the United States of America, 1989), p. 39.

4. Ibid., pp. 49–52.

5. Ibid., pp. 55–56.

CHAPTER 8
TOWARD CHRISTIAN CHARACTER

1. *Girl Scouts Survey on the Beliefs and Moral Values of America's Children* (New York: Girl Scouts of the United States of America, 1989), p. xiv.

2. Ibid.

3. Ibid., p. 23.

4. George Gallup, Jr., and Jim Castelli, *The People's Religion* (New York: Macmillan Publishing Co., 1989), pp. 16, 21.

5. *Girl Scouts Survey*, p. 56.

6. Gordon W. Allport, *The Nature of Prejudice* (Boston: Beacon Press, 1954), pp. 451–456.

7. Albert A. Harrison, *Individuals and Groups: Understanding Social Behavior.* (Monterey, Calif.: Brooks-Cole Publishing Co., 1976), pp. 415–419. For a critique of the Milgram experiment, yet support for the major findings, see Rom Harré, *Social Being* (Totowa, N.J.: Rowman & Littlefield, 1979), pp. 104–106.

8. Victor Paul Furnish, *Theology and Ethics in Paul* (Nashville: Abingdon Press, 1968), pp. 86–87.

9. Ibid., pp. 84–85.

For Further Reading

These books were selected primarily because they are written for lay people and are designed to introduce the reader to Christian ethics or moral education.

Aleshire, Daniel O. *Faith Care: Ministering to All God's People Through the Ages of Life.* Philadelphia: Westminster Press, 1988.

Beach, Waldo. *Christian Ethics in the Protestant Tradition.* Atlanta: John Knox Press, 1988.

Birch, Bruce C., and Larry L. Rasmussen. *Bible and Ethics in the Christian Life.* Minneapolis: Augsburg Fortress, 1989.

Chazan, Barry. *Contemporary Approaches to Moral Education.* New York: Teachers College Press, Columbia University, 1985.

Dykstra, Craig R. *Vision and Character: A Christian Educator's Alternative to Kohlberg.* New York: Paulist Press, 1981.

Elias, John L. *Moral Education: Secular and Religious.* Malabar, Fla.: Robert E. Krieger Publishing Co., 1989.

Higginson, Richard. *Dilemmas: A Christian Approach to Moral Decision Making.* Louisville, Ky.: Westminster/John Knox Press, 1988.

Moran, Gabriel. *No Ladder to the Sky: Education and Morality.* San Francisco: Harper & Row, 1987.

Warren, Michael. *Youth, Gospel, Liberation.* San Francisco: Harper & Row, 1987.

Wogaman, J. Philip. *Christian Moral Judgment.* Louisville, Ky.: Westminster/John Knox Press, 1989.